MASTER

THE COMBAT SABER

MASTER

THE COMBAT SABER

How to Train and

Fight with the

Form of a

Samurai

N R Burk

GREAT DAD MEDIA

Non-Fiction | Sports | Fencing

Permission requests to legally use this material in an academic setting and inquiries into discounts on bulk orders may be made through the Rogue Saber Academy:

https://www.roguesaber.com/contact.php

Published by Great Dad Media

www.GreatDadMedia.com

ISBN: 978-0-9996846-0-3 (eBook)
ISBN: 978-0-9996846-1-0 (Paperback)

First Edition • Published in 2017
Cover art by Connie Burk
Editing by Rebecca Ray

DISCLAIMER

This fencing guide (primarily of dueling techniques inspired by the Japanese martial arts of Kendo, Kenjutsu, and Iaido) is not an official publication of Lucasfilm Ltd., the Disney Corporation, or any of their affiliates. Nor is this guide connected to any official Kendo Federation or Japanese martial arts organization. The author is not, nor is the publisher, endorsed by or affiliated with these organizations.

The term "saber" is used herein to refer to the "combat saber" (described later in detail), and should not be confused with the fencing sabre, cavalry saber, any official trademarked words or products of Lucasfilm Ltd., the Disney Corporation, or any of their affiliates, or any of their Intellectual Property, including the mythical weapon depicted within the various media of the Star Wars Franchise. This book makes reference to copyrighted material owned by Lucasfilm Ltd. LLC. These references are ancillary and are made strictly for academic purposes. No claim to the license or rights to such terms is being made by the author or publisher.

The implementation of the instruction herein is done at your sole risk. The author, publisher, and the Rogue Saber Academy (RSA) provide the information herein for educational purposes and are not responsible for any physical injury or damage of any kind that may occur as a result of reading the contents of this book. In all physical sport, there is a chance for injury. You (as the reader) acknowledge that even when the RSA's official Safety Standards are followed, injury can still be expected due to the nature of the sport itself. You therefore agree to take full practical and legal responsibility for your own safety when training, meeting with others, sparring, and when otherwise using the resources in (or referenced by) this book.

To my Freeman brothers

May these lessons aid you in your quests!

And to all creators and collectors

who have also found themselves

in the search for sparring partners

and training.

CONTENTS

INTRODUCTION

WELCOME TO THE WORLD of combat saber dueling! Are you ready to put that shiny new combat saber to good use? Granted, igniting it and seeing its space-age glow and electric hum is gratifying, but that is only the beginning...

If you are a student of a formal saber academy, a dueling club member, a lone wolf committed to self-study, or a master training an apprentice, then this guide has what you need! In the pages to come, you will access over 50 powerful dueling techniques and lessons on meditation. You will explore the astonishing legends, history, and timeless code of the samurai. If you would like to start your own community or school club, you now have tips on how to do that as well!

Rather than provide you with sword fighting techniques based off of movie- or fan-inspired movements, this book delivers high-quality historical Japanese maneuvers, with built-in proven efficacy. In fact, every single technique lists the specific skill in either Kendo, Kenjutsu, or Iaido on which it is based. With such an approach, you will be able to connect with the spectacular Japanese warrior culture. Soon you will become so skilled with the art that you will truly master the combat saber and defeat any who challenge you.

This manual was created by the Rogue Saber Academy (RSA) on behalf of any academy, dojo, or club that would like to use the instruction herein to supplement their own program, or as a basis for their instruction. (You're welcome!) All techniques herein belong to the RSA's FORM 1 set of lessons. Corresponding training videos and additional similar techniques may be found on the RSA's official website. If there is any confusion about a particular technique, feel free to contact the RSA or look into a corresponding video if it has been made available. The Rogue Saber Academy also features an interactive map that can be used to find sparring partners in your area and even host or join local tournaments! More information about the RSA is included in the chapter "Ways to Continue Your Training," near the end of this manual.

For readers who have not yet secured their own combat saber, there have never been so many great options! Buying recommendations and a growing list of links to major online vendors can be found on the RSA's saber-smiths webpage. After you have received your saber, please consider leaving a review on the same page for those who follow.

It is important to note that if your dueling instructor (Master, *Sensei*, or Teacher) gives you instruction that contradicts those found in this book, then it is your responsibility to follow your instructor. This guide exists to provide a reference and starting point. Academy, dojo, and club leaders are free to teach a modified version of it, if they desire.

As more dueling schools have popped up around the world, a new sport has exploded onto the scene. (For the most dedicated of duelists, it has even become a team sport.) It revolves around duelists clashing combat sabers, striking each other, and scoring points in a fierce competition. Rules to a number of versions of it can be found online. Therefore, one main purpose of this book is to find the commonalities among these different sets of rules and publish their similarities, in a step toward strengthening the combat saber community and assisting in its intense growth.

But what was the first spark that stimulated this worldwide interest in dueling techniques in the first place? It all began with a fledgling online market in the mid-2000s for a fan-made device with exceptional potential...

WHAT IS THE COMBAT SABER?

IF YOU HAVEN'T YET come across these fan-made marvels, then it is with great pleasure that the following brief primer is presented, along with some historical context.

In order to understand what the combat saber means to collectors and duelists today, one must first understand the archetypal weapon it represents. The sword is like no other weapon in history. It is found in our greatest myths and is oft wielded by the bravest of fiction's heroes. No other weapon has outlived it or outmatched it in its versatility, symbolic meaning, or connection to personal refinement, morality, and honor. It is employed in attack, as well as for defense. It is used in close combat and therefore requires a high degree of mental and physical discipline from its wielder. Swords were given names, and gifted as heirlooms. Ancient smiths, dedicated to age-old methods, forged these elegant creations in secrecy and in fierce competition. For their fine work, they were often hailed as something akin to wizards.

Over time, societies grew to look up to heroes wielding swords. A deep need grew within us to mimic their movements and share their stories—stories in which fate itself rested upon a single duel.

Entire wars were fought and empires fell with the clash of blades. As tempered steel was replaced on the battlefield with gunpowder and lead, the sword lived on in fiction, sport, and martial arts. The deadly military purpose of the sword evaporated, but its connection to self-mastery and honor remained. Sharp blades were replaced with wooden sparring staffs, modified electric foils, and even the bamboo *shinai*. Special armor was designed and worn by duelists to prevent injury. Swordsmanship evolved, but much of the symbolism and traditions remained.

Still, around the world, our thirst for epic stories was not satisfied. To read of heroes and their swashbuckling duels was one thing, but to see them in motion pictures was unparalleled. Of course, the distinction of the most popular onscreen sword belongs, without question, to the Jedi's lightsaber.

Hollywood's depictions of the samurai and sword-wielding heroes such as Robin Hood and the Three Musketeers resonated with many young fans, some of whom would go on to become successful filmmakers. George Lucas' concept of the "laser sword," the Jedi's weapon, brought an important icon of heroism and chivalry into his curious space drama. It was brought to life through the special effects of the groundbreaking company Industrial Light and Magic. Most notably, this impressive device was given other-worldly power, thanks to the amazing sound design of Ben Burtt. The lightsaber's glowing and vibrant energy blades, crackling, and hums, launched it to become the most famous weapon in all of cinema.

From its debut in 1977 to today, the Star Wars franchise has given rise to a new popular mythology, enjoyed, celebrated, and discussed around the world. The heroes and gods of Mount Olympus, the Knights of the Round Table, and the super-powered do-gooders of comic books have been joined by the colorful cast from a galaxy far, far away. We see ourselves as the heroes (and sometimes the villains) in these epic tales, and often wonder if we would make the right choice if we were in their situations. On a deep level, Star Wars inspires heroism in each of us. This desire to emulate great characters, combined with the wellspring of creativity that is inspired by good storytelling, has led to what we call the "combat saber."

It is in the combat saber that two of the sword's legacies are realized. A fan can use a physical sword to duel others, reviving the history and traditions of the past, and also emulate the heroes from great stories, internalizing the epic while wielding the most iconic weapon of the great monomyth.

With that context in mind, what is the combat saber? The answer comes in four parts:

1. **The Technical Definition**. The Combat Saber is a fandom-inspired unique work of modern craftsmanship, with a polycarbonate blade attached to a metallic (often aluminum) hilt that houses electronics that produce futuristic sounds and vivid colors (or the colored light alone) usually via LEDs. These sabers (also known in the community as LED Lightsabers or Stunt Lightsabers) are reinforced and made for dueling, and belong, strictly speaking, more to the category of sports equipment than anything else. It is a real weapon for dueling and the result of impressive recent technological innovations. These are not the official merchandise of Lucasfilm or Disney, nor do they claim to be. These are either bought in pieces and assembled by the consumer or made available completed by saber-smiths and various online vendors.

2. **A Fan Collectible**. From the perspective of Star Wars fans, the Combat Saber is the realization of a dream. Unlike toys or costume props, these devices mimic the dueling capabilities and look and feel of their movie counterparts with stunning proficiency, especially when additional electronics are added that sense and respond to contact and movement. As an added bonus, anyone can handle these sabers without the fear of losing a limb or burning their homes down (a claim that cannot be made by those attempting to engineer laser-swords in concept rather than in application). Interestingly enough, the most recent Star Wars filmmakers have used similar props in the hands of actors to aid in the special effects process. They are a long awaited prize, made by fans, for fans. Yet you'll soon see that they have proven to become even more than that.

3. **Sports Equipment**. In terms of sports or martial arts, the Combat Saber is an adaptation of the electronic foil, sabre, or epee in Western traditions as well as the *bokken* or *shinai* in Eastern traditions. It can been seen as an evolution of sports equipment, moving further away from a sharp-edged and pointed metal to a less dangerous, though no less sturdy, material. In the blink-and-you-miss-it nature of fencing, a saber's glowing blade also provides many benefits to the duelists and to the audience, especially when the blades are of contrasting colors. After all, these weapons were originally conceptualized for entertainment. In order to capitalize on the unique spectacle these sabers create, many collectors tend to participate in choreographed performances in addition to their genuine duels.

4. **A Modern Sword**. The combat saber, in many ways, is the culmination of the many dueling swords of our ancestors. As in the case with the variations listed above, anyone with a desire to tap into the traditions of the past may use weapons with some major variances from historical blades and still be symbolically considered "swords." For example, it would be seen as both disrespectful and in violation of the rules for a duelist in kendo to hold their *shinai* by its "blade." Likewise, a combat saber duelist may treat their saber as a fan collectible, but also as sports equipment and as a modern sword. It is a link to the mythological, the sport, and also the historical; thus appropriate respect is shown.

The deadly *katana* was replaced by the *bokutō* for training, later to become the *shinai* for non-fatal combat in kendo. Kendo techniques were followed in the Star Wars films, and today, with any luck, you hold a combat-ready saber in your hands. You now have almost everything you need to engage in the sport of Combat Saber Dueling! Yet before we jump into the rules of the sport, the following chapter provides a few tips for new students.

GETTING STARTED

ALL STUDENTS OF THE COMBAT SABER, no matter their particular training program or affiliation, can benefit a great deal from the online resources provided by the Rogue Saber Academy. These resources are explored in greater detail later. If you have not yet created an account with the RSA, be sure to do so. It is a great way to officially begin your training. You will also be able to track your progress through the lessons to come, win digital prizes, and interact with other students who can help you along your path. Be sure to take a brief moment to create a new account here:

https://www.roguesaber.com/registrationform.php

Taking the first step on your journey is something to celebrate and share. But there is much to learn. As soon as you are ready to move on, you'll be directed to consider your own "Driving Force" and the common beginner mistakes you will be able to avoid.

Your Driving Force

At this point in their studies, all students are encouraged to take a moment to find and contemplate their own Driving Force. It is the fuel behind a champion's conquest. It is the confidence behind an elderly master's patience. If you enjoy engaging in meditations, this can certainly be a topic of such deep contemplation.

Learning any new worthwhile skill takes a good deal of sustained work, and the mastery of fencing techniques is no different. What separates the great duelists from all others? It is their dedication. A good way to unlock such dedication within yourself is to identify what truly drove you to begin your training in the first place. Is it your sense of adventure? Is it the natural high that comes from competing in such a sport? Is it the thrill of discovery? Or is it perhaps the timeless sense of belonging that comes from making a physical connection to the past? Only you can discover and hold onto your Driving Force. Doing so will unleash your true potential!

Top 10 Beginner Mistakes

Perhaps you have waved a saber or two around before. You may have even engaged in a few duels with a younger sibling or classmate. You may be asking yourself, "Why should I study samurai inspired sword lessons when I am already pretty good in a fight?"

In a way, this question answers itself. For the most part, we no longer live in an age in which skill with the sword determines the outcome of a war, or resolves some challenge to one's honor. Therefore, the average person isn't expected to be a proficient fencer. It follows then, that the majority of people you meet have only a superficial level of aptitude when it comes to sword fighting. Why should you study? Because diving into even the first few lessons herein will give you a substantial advantage against almost all opponents you will face.

Of course, there are deeper reasons to acquaint oneself with the noble teachings of traditional swordsmanship. You'll soon realize that they have almost nothing to do with sport, or even the weapon itself. Read on, and you'll come to understand these deeper reasons.

Several students begin their training, but few complete it. Just like with many things in life, it is easy to spot who has taken their lessons seriously and who has not. To give you an idea of the mistakes that give away your "beginner" status, here are the top ten common mistakes made by the untrained duelist:

1. **Targeting Blades**: An untrained duelist will swing to hit the blade of their opponent, time and time again. How do such duelists think the match will end, and how can a winner be determined? When you duel, target the person, not their saber.

2. **The Double-Knockout**: Uninitiated fencers can be amusing to watch. More often than not, they will both grow tired of the endless clash of blades, and summon the courage to

attack. Alas, they both fail to think things through, and they end up striking each other at the same time. How can you hit your opponent without getting hit? It takes study and practice to find out.

3. **Uncoordinated Footwork**: When an advanced duelist is challenged by a newcomer, this tends to be the downfall of the latter. They swing their saber about, not being able to match their swordwork with their step. This leads to being unbalanced, awkward, and constantly having to re-adjust their footing when they should be fencing.

4. **Ignored Body Language**: "Telegraphing" is when one fencer unintentionally signals to the other what they are going to do, before they do it. It is a key form of body language that many fail to consider in a sport like this. Worse still, the untrained fail to pick up on these important hints, even when their opponent broadcasts them loud and clear.

5. **All Style and No Substance**: Did you think your fancy flourishes and flips would endear you to the crowd? Unfortunately, duelists who place performance over practicality don't last long in a duel, giving up their fans to more proficient opponents. It is a good thing that modern fencing techniques have been refined over the centuries into what works best, granting you the tools you need to stay in the fight.

6. **A Lack of Safety Measures**: Do you remember what it feels like to get a blade slapped right across your fingers? Combat sabers may look great, but they can pack a punch. The next time you see newbies sparring in the park without even a pair of gloves, let them know that a little body armor can go a long way.

7. **Slow and Sloppy Strikes**: Take a moment to watch an Olympic fencing match, or an international kendo competition. What do you see? For most new students, it is surprising just how lightning fast each strike is delivered. Full intent, dedication, and quick action are all the marks of a skilled swordsman.

8. **Being Constantly Compromised**: It can be daunting for new students when they see how much time is needed to learn proper posture, grip, footwork, and the other small details of fencing. Frankly, all of these things are important, because making a successful strike isn't enough. It is common to see shiny new duelists force themselves into compromising positions at every turn, due to a lack of proper technique. Their missteps become their opponents' opportunities.

9. **Endless Practice and No Improvement**: It is terribly frustrating to see dedicated veteran duelists fail to defeat younger and less experienced opponents. Many are slow to learn that not all techniques are created equal, and practicing sub-par maneuvers will still result in sub-par performance, no matter how many hours were spent on practice and mastery.

10. **A Failure to Plan Ahead**: Finally, the last and most common mistake made by the untrained duelist is that of a lack of thinking things through. After you target your opponent's arm, how will you avoid their counter-attack? If your opponent knocks your blade to the side, how will you respond? A skilled duelist can answer all of these kinds of questions quickly and fittingly.

Are you tired of making these beginner mistakes? With even a small amount of the training found in this manual, you'll be able to bedazzle the crowds, connect with the great swordsmen of the past, and secure satisfying victories. At the very least you can be sure that your power in a duel will dramatically increase, and that new awesome combat saber you've collected will finally be put to good use.

THE SPORT OF COMBAT SABER DUELING

THERE IS A NEW SPORT rapidly growing in popularity, primarily among fans of the Star Wars franchise. Interestingly, it is also quickly gaining momentum among martial arts enthusiasts, fencing clubs, and the lovers of new alternative sports (such as College Quidditch, and Archery Tag). The construction of these high-end combat sabers has become a highly competitive and lucrative industry. No longer are we content to admire the glowing light. We want to spar with our friends, challenge other duelists, and become the greatest of champions!

Each Academy, Dojo, and Club may have its own special variation on the following rules. However, if you would like to get a general idea of what to expect from the new sport of Combat Saber Dueling, you've come to the right place. The most up-to-date version of the following rules and safety standards may be found on the RSA's website.

Basic Rules of the Sport

The Agreement. Both opponents must have agreed before the commencement of a match on the following rules and on the amount of "points" (or successful strikes) to be earned first by the winner (typically five). In a tournament, the tournament organizer may set the winning amount of points for each round. It is also determined whether or not helmets or body armor will be worn. The appointment of a judge is optional. A judge may be any person familiar with these rules, whose authority is accepted by both duelists before the match.

The Weapons. Both opponents must possess standard combat-ready sabers in good repair. These are sabers with reinforced blades to prevent shattering or denting on impact. Their hilts must contain electronics to at least successfully illuminate the blades. Their blades must be between 24" (about 60 cm) and 36" (about 90 cm) in length (not including the hilt). If detachable, blades must be properly fastened to the hilt, and connective mechanisms must be tightened before and during a spar or duel as needed. The blades must be illuminated ("ignited" or "armed") during a successful strike, for a point to be made. Either Duelist may be armed with one saber, two sabers, sabers with hand guards, saber-staffs containing two blades, or sabers with abnormally long hilts.

Safety Measures. Both opponents understand that minor injury will most likely take place. Nevertheless, proper safety precautions must be taken to avoid serious injury. The match must be located in a publicly accessible area with plenty of space for movement and moderate pedestrian traffic. Should pedestrians disrupt the match, it should immediately be paused and later resumed. A duelist is not permitted to physically, or through lack of proper warning, back an opponent into any obstacle. All sabers are to be held firmly to avoid a hilt slipping out of one's hands. If a duelist is male, he should wear a cup or jock strap for protection. Both duelists should wear protective gloves and shoes or boots. The use of mouth guards and eye protection is strongly recommended. If it is agreed that strikes to the head will be allowed, helmets must be worn by both duelists. If it is agreed that stabbing techniques will be allowed, suitable body armor must be worn by both duelists. Additionally, the RSA's Official Safety Standards (provided below), are to be strictly followed in their entirety.

The Bow and Salute. Opponents face each other and ignite their sabers. They stand only close enough to allow a few inches of space between the tips of their sabers as they are pointed toward each other with extended arms. Both combatants bow and salute each other. The bow is quick and respectful, at roughly a 30° angle. The salute can be a simple spin, flourish, or signature flourish of the saber, while respectful eye contact is maintained. Thus the match begins. This sequence is also to be followed if a match is resumed after any break.

Earning Points. One point is earned by a duelist if he/she lands a strike on the opponent. A "strike" is a successful attack in which the blade has made contact with the opponent's hands, body, or armor, or if the opponent's own blade makes contact with his/her own hands, body, or armor. Strikes to the eyes, face, throat, groin, or knees must be avoided at all costs, and do not yield points. If helmets are not worn, head strikes are also prohibited. A stabbing strike in the absence of body armor is also illegal and yields no point. Grabbing one's own blade or the saber of an opponent is not allowed. Likewise, punches, holds, grabbing, kicks, and hitting an opponent with a saber's hilt are all illegal actions.

The Boundaries. The match takes place in a "starting area," roughly in the center of the "dueling area," which has clearly established and agreed upon boundaries. (These boundaries must follow visible markers such as painted lines, trees, walls, fences, etc.) Either duelist may not retreat both feet beyond the pre-determined boundaries of the dueling area. If this occurs, one point is awarded to the duelist remaining inside the boundaries, and both must suspend the match, return to the starting area, and salute again before resuming. All points earned thus far remain.

Self-Declaration. In the moment a point is earned, the duelist who was hit calls out the number of points so far earned by their opponent. For example, if this was your opponent's second point made against you, you would call out, "two." There is no formal break in the action, as the match continues unabated. If a disagreement arises, it is settled with the ruling of an appointed judge or with a coin-toss.

Halting For Injury. All care and precautions should be taken in order to avoid injury. If a duelist is seriously injured, or otherwise in need of an emergency respite, they will raise their hand, with palm toward their opponent in a universal "stop" motion. This will signal to both duelists (and perhaps judges and audience members as well) that the active spar or duel is now temporarily suspended. Both players will then agree on the proper course of action. If the match is to continue, the duelists will return to the starting area, bow, and salute.

Claiming Victory and Conclusion. The spar or duel is over when one duelist first reaches the previously agreed upon number of points. If both players reach that number of points at the same time, the match is a draw and would be recorded as a "tied match." After the match, both duelists honorably agree upon and accept the results of the duel, deactivate their sabers, shake hands, and go their separate ways. These results are then reported within 72 hours after the event by each duelist if it is to count toward their progress within an academy or club.

Basic Safety Standards

Personal Responsibility. In all physical sport, there is a chance for injury. As a public service, these safety standards were written to give further protocols designed to minimize the chance of injury and promote safety and wellbeing for all involved when engaging in the sport of Combat Saber Dueling. All users of the RSA's online media, resources, and published works (referred to as "students" or "duelists") acknowledge that even when the following standards are applied, minor injury can still be expected due to the nature of the sport itself. In accepting the RSA's Terms and Conditions, all students agree to take full practical and legal responsibility for their own safety when training, meeting with others, and so forth.

Personal Health Practices. It is recommended that all students engage in thirty minutes of rigorous cardio exercise (or proper weight-lifting) for at least thirty minutes a day, five days a week, prior to and during their combat saber training. This exercise, in combination with plenty of water intake and healthy nutritional habits, can prevent a number of injuries. Students should actively seek to increase their physical endurance, strength, and flexibility. If serious illness or other health concerns arise, students are expected to cancel any scheduled event in which they are to participate, in order to adequately recover and prevent the spread of disease to other students. To avoid injury before a match, duelists should stretch all major muscle groups and warm up with a quick jog or exercise routine.

Assembling a First Aid Kit. It is expected that all students arrive at their matches with a small first aid kit contained within a waterproof container. This kit should be well-stocked with materials such as: common adhesive bandages, general disinfectant, hand sanitizer, insect bite ointment, cleaning wipes, finger splints, a roll of first aid tape, sterile pads and gauze rolls, vinyl gloves, scissors, and a note with the phone numbers of nearby hospitals and the local police.

What To Bring. It is recommended that all students bring with them to each match one or more personal water bottles, their first aid kit, and a working cell phone. Wearing lotion-style sunblock with both UVA and UVB protection and an SPF above 15 is highly recommended. In addition to the protective materials given in the official sport rules, all duelists should wear clothing appropriate for the weather. Watches and jewelry should be removed prior to any spar or duel.

The Importance of a Second. Students should never go to a scheduled match or tournament alone. A "second" is traditionally a fellow duelist who is expected to engage in the match on behalf of a fallen comrade. However, the RSA uses this term to mean a well-known and trusted friend of the duelist who is to accompany them to a match, ensure that all rules and safety standards are followed, and contact help in the event of an emergency. The mere presence of an attentive second may also dissuade criminality at or near the match. A second can serve as a judge and also help to ensure both duelists are not behaving too aggressively or carelessly. They should never be engaged in a duel (or other distracting activity) at the same time as the duelist with whom they arrived to the match. Following the match, both duelists, along with their seconds, should go their separate ways.

Interactions With Other Students. Online, or in person, a student should not give their full real name, home address, or contact information to another student. Before any event, a duelist should contact family members or friends to let them know where they are expected to be and when they expect to return. If a match has been scheduled between two duelists who are unfamiliar with each other, both participants and their seconds should be alert at all times for unusual behavior, ready to cancel the event and go their separate ways at the earliest suspicion. For example, once duelists meet at the agreed-upon meeting location, they should never go to a second, unplanned location. The suggestion to carry out the match in a way contrary to the public plans for that match should be cause to cancel the event.

Proper Dueling Techniques. All students should study and practice a great deal before engaging in a match. (The RSA's training lessons, in particular, have been designed to grant students with technical advantages and also to help them develop safe habits. Therefore, adherence to the steps of each technique taught is important.) To avoid injury, control of a duelist's weapon must take priority over speed or style. Consequently, all duelists are strongly encouraged to only duel or spar at 50% of their maximum possible speed and intensity. A focus on maintaining control, preventing harm, and performing at one's best, takes far more skill than reckless dueling. Someone who trains with this kind of focus will not only be a safer duelist, but will also benefit from greater self-discipline along the way.

A Comparison With Kendo

After you have properly learned and practiced the techniques taught in this book, you will have developed into a force to be reckoned with against any other combat saber duelist—even those from alternative training backgrounds. Dedicated research, testing, and development has all gone into creating this manual with that goal in mind.

Should this manual be considered an introductory course to iaido, kenjutsu, or (more particularly) kendo? Academically, yes, but not in practice. If you master the lessons herein and compete with a master of these traditional Japanese martial arts according to the rules of Combat Saber Dueling, you would both be on near-equal footing, and the competition would be fierce. However, if this scenario were reversed, and you engaged in a kendo match with only the training from this book, then you will find yourself often foiled in the different landscape of kendo's specific rules, standards, and approach to dueling.

If you do move on to formally learn kendo after mastering these techniques (something highly encouraged by the author), then you must approach your new school with completely new eyes and humbly enter as an entirely new student. The same would be true if you move on to learn Western fencing, or even study under a different academy. As you train, the similarities will gradually become apparent, and only then will you be able to tap into the wealth of skills previously learned.

Kendo has powerfully influenced the creation of the sport of Combat Saber Dueling. Yet before anyone gets too carried away with comparisons between the two disciplines, it is important to note some key differences:

Cultural Emphasis: Many terms for the techniques, movements, objects, and procedures in kendo have only Japanese names. It is often the case that no attempt has been made to translate these elements into any other language. This reflects how kendo serves a deep purpose beyond that of mere fencing instruction. Kendo embodies a cultural heritage, dripping with meaning, with tangible ties to the historic samurai. Combat Saber Dueling, much like the beloved Star Wars franchise, contrasts this by drawing inspiration from several different cultures and disciplines.

Strict Rules and Regulations: Every aspect of kendo is regulated and demands strict adherence to uniform rules. For example, practitioners of kendo follow set steps in putting on their *bōgu* (body armor), even before a match. In contrast, the rules of Combat Saber Dueling are, by design, less numerous and less specific, in order to serve the greatest number of academies, clubs, and dojos around the world.

Body Armor: In competitions, kendo practitioners sport heavy samurai-inspired armor. Duelists can then take a heavy beating, with strikes to the head (and other vulnerable areas) with full force. Male saber duelists wear groin protection, and all saber duelists wear gloves. Additional gear is optional and utilized on a case-by-case basis to allow for a greater variety of techniques that can safely be used.

Target Zones: In Combat Saber Dueling, almost every part of the body is a valid target, and the use of helmets and body armor are optional as long as the techniques they protect against are not used. Points can be earned in kendo by striking the top of the head, the wrists, the throat, or the flank. Of course, strikes to the head and throat are only allowable because of the protective *bōgu*.

The Weapons: The bamboo *shinai* is light in weight and offers a slick wooden surface along its blade with a padded tip. It is modeled after the *katana* and is specifically optimized for use in kendo. The combat saber is, by comparison, heavy with an even slicker glass surface along its blade with a rounded, flat, or pointed tip. In addition, its hilt is metallic and may give its wielder something of a workout with enough use. It is originally inspired by the weapons of the Jedi in the Star Wars franchise, although many are now being made with the sole purpose of dueling with this sport in mind. Given this added weight and design, a combat saber duelist should exercise much greater control and restraint in order to avoid injury.

Valid Strikes: In kendo, a strike is only considered valid, and a point is awarded, if the strike satisfies the high standards of proper *kiai* (intense shouting), correct posture and footwork, and appropriate seriousness and attitude. In addition to these and other requirements, the correct edge and part of the *shinai* must also have made contact at an adequate speed. It goes without saying that skilled duelists in kendo may flail on each other all day long without scoring a satisfactory point. A combat saber duelist, however, can offhandedly graze the arm of an opponent with their blade and be awarded a point. This is a call back to the initial inspiration for the device, treating it as if it were a controlled burning blade of energy that could cut, melt, and singe in any direction upon contact.

Winning a Match: Valid strikes are declared, and points are awarded, by a number of judges, and once two valid points are scored, a match in kendo is set. In Combat Saber Dueling, the number of points that lead to a victory is decided upon by the duelists before each match. Typically, a valid strike is declared by the duelist who has been struck.

Footwear: While combat saber duelists compete with protective shoes or boots, kendo practitioners glide along the dojo's floor in bare feet.

The Salute and Bow: A practice session or match begins much differently in kendo, and often includes both opponents sinking low in *sonkyo*. Various movements such as the "signature flourish" serve a similar purpose in Combat Saber Dueling.

An entire book could be filled with these differences, but suffice it to say that they are numerous. Although kendo techniques can be utilized with great success in this new sport, the rules of Combat Saber Dueling are radically different from those in kendo. Hopefully, no student of this manual alone will ever make the mistake of claiming to be proficient in kendo, or even in kenjutsu or iaido. However, a student of this manual will come away with a much higher-than-average understanding of these Japanese arts, and the history and culture that gave rise to them.

THE AGE OF THE SAMURAI

EACH SWORD-FIGHTING SKILL you learn from this manual is based upon the martial arts of either kendo, kenjutsu, and/or Iaido. These Japanese forms have been tried and tested over centuries, and further refined into techniques we can employ.

Today, sword fighting itself (in all of its forms) is a connection to history. This is an unbreakable link, and speaks to an inherent responsibility for all who take up the sword. But to which history are you connecting? No student of these ancient arts can truly master them without a working understanding of the legends and lessons behind them. Therefore, in this section you will get an idea of the elite warrior class that grasped and maintained power through these techniques—the samurai!

The age of the samurai spans over 1,000 years of a rich history of honor, betrayal, war, and strategy. Typically, to be a samurai, one must have three things:

1. A master, clan leader, emperor, *Shogun* (military dictator), or *Daimyō* (feudal lord) to whom allegiance, loyalty, and service is sworn. (Warriors without a master were known as *rōnin*.)

2. A fierce dedication to the lifestyle and code of honor of Japanese warriors, known as *Bushido* (explored in a later chapter).

3. Exceptional skills and training. (A samurai was not simply a swordsman, but often wrote poetry, mastered archery, and hosted tea ceremonies.)

Alternatively, being born into the samurai class at certain times in history also automatically allowed one to take upon themselves the title. In other times, one could only legally become a samurai through birthright.

Much of what we often think of the samurai in modern times has no doubt been romanticized and amalgamated with the similarly romanticized knights of medieval Europe. Therefore, the cautious historian may want to exercise a degree of healthy skepticism when studying this subject. With that said, the following treatment represents only a high level summary of much of Japan's history surrounding the noble warrior class, peppered with traditional stories and legends. These legends are told with some embellishment in order to bring the narrative into some harmony with conflicting sources. At times, multiple legends have been merged and told as a single story. It is the intention and priority of the author to convey the spirit behind each story, providing a small taste of culture, to enrich the historical narrative.

The epic to come has been divided according to three historic periods. The first, Ancient and Classical Japan, sets the stage for the budding nation and its traditional emperor. The second period, Medieval Japan, begins with the stories of the fearless *bushi*, the spiritual and literal predecessors of the samurai and the wars of rivaling familial clans. The third period, Early Modern Japan, encapsulates the legendary rise of the Samurai class and the conversion of their ways into the martial arts that live on today.

Ancient and Classical Japan

In the year 660 BCE (about 100 years after the first Olympic Games in Greece and about 100 years before the birth of Confucius), the oldest continual hereditary monarchy in the world began. That's right, the imperial house of Japan is over 2,675 years old, and is still intact today!

For generations, the royal family ruled over the country. But it hasn't always been in power. By the **Kofun period** (250–538 CE), the emperor had unified most of the region under his (and sometimes her) rule. Through conquest, and occasionally by peaceful means, the emperor assimilated surrounding regions into the "Yamato state."

Hundreds of years under the rule of the imperial family, however, would come to an abrupt end at the hands of a new family, harboring foreign beliefs. By the dawn of the **Asuka period** (538–710 CE), Buddhism had been introduced to the region to contend with the native traditions. A Buddhist family, the Soga clan, overthrew the government, and it is in their writings that the kingdom is first described as the "land of the rising sun." This iconic description would live on in the identity of the future nation of Japan, as seen in its national flag today.

At this time, the Japanese people were ruled from the capital city of Asuka. Historians, therefore, conventionally use the capital city's name to identify this period. This technique is helpful, since the years to come are filled with great and terrible usurpers who strategically move the capital to a new city soon after claiming political power.

In the year 645 the shockingly powerful Fujiwara clan overthrew the Soga clan in a surprise coup. The Fujiwaras were not content to merely rule, but were eager to reshape the laws of the land under the influence of Confucianism. They implemented the Taika Reforms and the Taihō Code, expanding the government in ways that paralleled a number of Chinese patterns and philosophies. High taxes were demanded of land owners, slowly impoverishing many small farmers who now had to work for wealthier land owners. To keep the peace, the imperial army was mostly filled by the nation's citizens through mandatory conscription. These new laws would forever alter the course of Japan's history, setting the stage for the distant samurai to come.

The Fujiwara moved the capital to Heijō-kyo (Nara), starting off the **Nara period** (710–794). It is at this time that the hints of a new trend can be seen in how the emperor ruled. Rather than act as a common ruler or dictator, commanding armies and managing the country's policies, the Japanese imperial family took upon themselves a new obsession—art. (It is possible that this new obsession may be a critical factor in the longevity of the imperial line.)

For the next 500 years, poetry, luxury, literature, and other cultural pursuits became the priority of the imperial court. In 711 the *Kojiki*, one of the most ancient documents of Japanese mythology, was written. It contributes many elements to the Shinto belief system, a faith that honors Japan's emperor as a descendant of the gods, and one that would eventually become the dominant religion of the region.

Yet public faith in the divine ruler may have wavered considerably at the time. Small pox and a number of natural disasters dramatically reduced Japan's population. Perhaps, as a consequence, Buddhism became much more widely practiced among the aristocracy.

While the emperor mused and painted, a great deal of power gradually shifted to local leaders, leading to a sizable drop in taxes flowing to the emperor over time. Following Chinese tradition, these local leaders employed principled and well-qualified servants—the early samurai. Indeed, this is where the samurai get their name, literally translating into "those who serve" or "retainers." Yet these early servants may not have even been armed. Warriors were at that time referred to as *Bushi*, the root word of the way of the warrior, *Bushido*.

The slow decentralization of the government left a growing void that others were eager to fill. The first to step up were the warrior monks of the new Buddhist monasteries (conveniently exempt from paying the high taxes) that dotted the capital city. They had become very popular and influential but were held at bay by the imperial army. By 792, however, the emperor was facing an even greater crisis.

In addition to the Buddhist monasteries, the growing estates of wealthy nobles were also tax exempt, dealing a crippling blow to the emperor's treasury. The scant taxes flowing into his court were no longer sufficient to pay his troops. Many highly-trained imperial warriors, successful in their mission to subdue the native Emishi people to the north, were either dismissed or left the imperial court of their own accord to seek out their fortunes. Citizens were no longer required to join the army, and the imperial forces diminished considerably.

In order to preserve the emperor's court, the capital was first relocated to Nagaoka in 784, and finally to Heian (the city known today as Kyoto) in 794. This is where the imperial family would remain for over one thousand years.

It is in the **Heian period** (794–1185) that Chinese influence in art, music, and literature began to wane, and Japanese culture became more pronounced. Several masterpieces were created, some notably by aristocratic women. The social elites praised each other in their poetry for being sensitive, leisurely, and for living in a continuous state of melancholy. Yet this was also an era born in bubbling chaos. Economic and political failures arose. The country had reached a tipping point.

The head of the Fujiwara clan, a close ally of the imperial family, governed at this time as a *Kampaku* (regent). Yet without a strong military force to support the imperial magistrates (sent to govern and collect taxes), the *kampaku* lost control of the wealthy land owners, who would often consolidate power as familial clans. They had become independent and dangerous. Soon, familial clans owned more property and demanded more allegiance than the central government.

These wealthy clans hired their own private armies to repel the government's magistrates and to protect themselves from rivals. They turned to a new generation of skilled servants to lead their private armies, ones that were not only highly loyal, but also highly skilled in the arts of war. Some would emerge from among the farmers. Others had been discharged by the indifferent imperial court. These were the new elite warriors, a hybrid of the servant and the *bushi*. These were the samurai.

To equip the samurai, over 450 blademakers dotted the landscape in the Heian period, continuing the forging traditions passed down for generations. Some historians believe that these traditions were born in Japan, while others assert that they most likely first evolved in China and crossed through Korea before recorded history.

By 1016, the strategic and powerful leaders of the Fujiwara clan had passed their peak of political influence. At the same time, two fast-growing samurai clans (the Taira and Minamoto), with distant familial ties to the imperial family, had been consolidating power. The Taira clan in particular had been filling key governmental positions, allying with independent clans, and raising large armies. The government had called upon the Taira and Minamoto to suppress rebellions against the Abe and Kiyohara clans, and again in 1156 between the contested heirs to the throne. In the chaos, the Taira rose up against the Minamoto clan and defeated them! They seized control over the government, and demanded recognition from the imperial family as Japan's new rulers.

Thus began the reign of military leaders, or "Bakufu," over the land. The emperor agreed to publically recognize the new military leader as the true ruler. In return, the military leader allowed the imperial bloodline to continue in Kyoto. The imperial family was stripped of any real power, and the precedent was set that would be followed for generations. True political and militaristic leadership was granted to the mightiest of samurai, whose ways would dramatically influence Japanese society for the next 700 years.

The betrayal at the hands of the Taira gave rise to a bloody feud. The Minamoto rebounded against the Taira in the Heiji Rebellion in 1160 but were defeated again. Some of their leaders were executed, and others were banished to Kamakura. The Minamoto united again and battled the Taira for four years in the epic Genpei War. A legendary hero in that war came to be known as one of the greatest samurai of all time—Minamoto Yoshitsune.

The Legend of Minamoto Yoshitsune

Yoshitsune's father had supported the Taira clan in the Hōgen Rebellion but would come to regret it in its aftermath. He spoke out against the regime and was promptly assassinated! His eldest sons were killed, and his wife and remaining children were assigned to a Taira clan official. The official spared them but separated the children and sent Yoshitsune to a Buddhist monastery. Local folklore has it that while Yoshitune was being raised by the monks, he would sneak off to train with a secret teacher, Sōjōbō, who helped him master the art of the sword atop mount Kurama.

Years later, a traveling Yamabushi monk visited Yoshitsune's monastery. This monk learned all he could from every monastery he visited, and he was chillingly good with the blade. He carried a large collection of swords, one from every foe he had bested in combat. He wore a black cap, and his name was Benkei. By the time he encountered the 15 year old Yoshitune, his reputation hadn't been tarnished by a single loss.

Once he heard of Benkei's boisterous challenges, Yoshitsune retrieved his own trusted blade and rushed to meet the traveler. The two young men dueled during the ensuing storm. Each clash sent sparks that vanished in the rain. Yet, even as Benkei eyed this next sword for his collection, Yoshitsune defeated him. The surrounding monks were hushed in astonishment. Immediately, Benkei pledged his loyalty to the prodigy as his retainer, and the two became fast friends, teaching each other all they knew. Word quickly spread of this formidable swordsman, the one who bested Benkei, a possible threat to the reigning Taira.

Yoshitsune escaped from the region, with Benkei as his right-hand man. They found shelter in the Mutsu province with Governor Fujiwara Hidehira of the Northern Fujiwara clan. Hidehira was impressed with Yoshitsune. He could see that the boy would one day become a great leader. Hidehira gave him a place to live and the means by which he could continue his training.

In 1180, Prince Mochihito, of the powerless imperial family, published a bold statement, calling upon the Minamoto clan to set things right and overtake the Taira. Many answered and began to assemble, but they received news that the prince had been killed just weeks after making the call to arms.

Yoshitsune knew his time had come. He once again took up his family name and joined with the rising armies in the Kanto region. It was only then that, as men, he and his older brother Yoritomo were finally reunited. To his brother and clan, Yoshitsune pledged his loyalty and his sword. It was decided that their clan would take the fight directly to the capital city, Kyoto.

However, before they could mobilize, their power-hungry cousin, Minamoto Yoshinaka, would betray his clan, leaving all others behind in a rush to the capital. The Taira leaders strategically retreated into their mountain stronghold of Ichi-no-Tani, allowing Yoshinaka to overtake Kyoto with ease. Boasting of his skill, Yoshinaka took the throne for himself, imprisoned the emperor, and assumed the title of "Lord Kiso." Lord Kiso soon after stretched his forces thin, attempting to conquer more of the surrounding regions. His ambition outreached his skill, he failed to instill loyalty in his troops, and his cousins knew it.

Yoshitsune joined his brother on the dangerous mission to oust the greedy Lord Kiso. At the sight of the terrible samurai army crossing the bridges into the capital during the Battle of Awazu, Kiso's forces fled in terror. They were pursued until they could retreat no more. Kiso himself abandoned his throne, protected only by his lady samurai, Tomoe Gozen, who is often described as an attractive woman with long dark hair. She was renowned as a deadly accurate archer, on foot and horseback, and she defeated much larger and stronger samurai with a single slice from her sword. In the Battle of Awazu, she fought bravely on the front lines.

When he knew his defeat was nigh, Kiso sent Tomoe Gozen away from the battle, insisting that he desired to die only among his brothers. With the imperial capital reclaimed, Yoshitsune gained the respect of his clan, as well as that of the rescued emperor.

Yoshitsune and his samurai were then sent to defeat the Taira forces at the mountain stronghold of Ichi-no-Tani. It was surrounded by protective forts and was backed against a steep cliff. Before the forts could be readied for battle, Yoshitsune and the Miamoto forces split up and took them in the dead of night. While the Taira warriors, assured of their victory, pushed out to meet his samurai, Yoshitsune personally led his best men down the cliffside in a daring feat of terror to attack Ichi-no-Tani head-on. He captured the stronghold, entrapping the Taira clan forces.

As he and Benkei led thousands of samurai to victory in a number of battles against the Taira, Yoshitsune would rise in popularity. It was his fierce loyalty, skill, and honor that demanded respect from his men, and earned him the rank of general, as well as other honors within his clan. At times he was trusted with governing from Kyoto as deputy, in the stead of his brother. From there he issued popular decrees such as one that restricted lords from demanding higher taxes from the lower classes without his brother's consent. His victories throughout the Genpei War inspired his troops and his people. Even the cloistered emperor had great respect for him, and named Yoshitsune as the General of Iyo.

Yet in Kajiwara Kagetoki's eyes, (Yoritomo's most trusted retainer) the younger brother had become a bit too popular. Upon his return to Kyoto, Yoritomo stripped Yoshitsune of his ranks and honors. Kagetoki insisted on sending Yoshitsune into the front lines, in the direst of conditions. When Yoshitsune would contend with him on strategy, Kagetoki would return to Yoritomo with slanders and rumors against the younger brother.

Nevertheless, Yoshitsune continued to fight gallantly. On the battlefield, he would follow the questionable orders from higher-up officials and still claim victory, against all odds. He and his men sailed against the enemy in vicious storms, when all others held back. His small band intimidated armies more than twice their size. As the word of each victory spread, troops and ships from across the region joined the cause, and the Minamoto clan grew in strength. In fact, in the Battle of Dan-no-ura, Yoshitsune inspired enemy generals to turn on the Taira clan, betraying the positions of their leaders. The changes in the tide were used to his advantage. In complete and terrible triumph, the Taira clan's leaders were captured and their remaining armies were driven into the sea.

What became of the armies defeated at the ocean's edge? According to local legends, they live on today as Heike Crabs whose carapaces closely resemble the scowl of the Taira warriors. The Battle of Dan-no-ura, however, inspired far more than legends. It started Japan on a course that would lead to a redefined political structure and a fundamental change to the role of the samurai.

When Yoshitsune arrived victorious with his prisoners to the new capital city, he was not allowed within its gates. The slanders and rumors against him had convinced his brother that Yoshitsune could not be trusted. In a desperate attempt to clear his name, Yoshitsune sent his famous "Koshigoe Letter," inside the city, protesting against each slur and asserting his loyalty to the Minamoto family and to Yoritomo in particular. Yet it was far too late. Those who defended him were exiled from the region, and Yoshitsune realized that his life was in danger, yet again.

Word reached Yoshitsune that the emperor supported him in the overthrow of his brother, yet this was never Yoshitsune's intention. Armies of samurai, still loyal to Yoshitsune, rallied behind him, but they were no match for the greater united Minamoto clan. They decided to flee to Kyushu, and were later forced to retreat to the western provinces. Samurai loyal to him defended his honor to their death, until Yoshitsune escaped with only a handful of retainers, living in exile in the hills south of Kyoto.

Keeping one step ahead of his brother's forces, he and Benkei returned to their old home in Mutsu, where their friend, Governor Fujiwara Hidehira, had died, leaving the governorship in his will to Yoshitsune. Yet those wishes would be dismissed by the Northern Fujiwara clan, who broke under pressure, and betrayed Yoshitsune's location to Yoritomo.

When his pursuers arrived in Mutsu in the Battle of Koromo River, the great Yoshitsune and his friend Benkei met their end honorably. After the death of his brother, Yoritomo continued on to slaughter and conquer the territory of the Northern Fujiwara clan.

• • •

As students of swordsmanship, we can learn from "The Legend of Minamoto Yoshitsune" that the greatest of warriors must passionately train and endure the rigors of training well. One must follow one's inner code of honor and make the most out of unfavorable circumstances. Perhaps most importantly, one must always be aware of the shifting power dynamics in battle and adjust one's strategy accordingly.

Medieval Japan

By the end of the Genpei War, the Minamoto clan was able to put an end to Taira supremacy. Minamoto Yoritomo succeeded as the leader of the land. He was born in the city where his clan's leaders had once been exiled, Kamakura, which would now be the true seat of government and military power during the **Kamakura period** (1185–1333). After eliminating all of his potential enemies, including several close family members, he was appointed as Shogun (high military officer) by the emperor. As it was the samurai that truly gave Yoritomo his power, he decreed that one may only become one of these great warriors with his authorization.

The golden age of the samurai had begun. Japan was now under a new feudal system. At its head was the hereditary military dictatorship, the Shogunate, supported by several wealthy and powerful lords (the *Gokenin*, and later the *Daimyōs*) who employed their private armies of samurai, now an elite social class. These elite warriors were the retainers of the lord's land and protectors of their legacy. Under the protection of the samurai were also the other classes, the farmers, artisans, and merchants.

It is in this era that Buddhism spread in prominence, no longer solely the philosophy of the elites. The emerging (and distinctly Japanese) Zen Buddhism, in particular, became incredibly popular among the warrior class. It supported and reinforced many tenets of *bushido*, promoted austere and simple rituals, and focused on self-discipline.

It was a time of the creation of elaborate poetry and epic tales of war. Historians also point to the Kamakura period as the time in which the sword became much more meaningful to the samurai, above the bow, staff, spear, or any of the other weapons with which the versatile warriors were proficient. The samurai more generally came to believe that the sword was the symbol of a man's honor, the vessel of his spirit, and the tool of self-perfection. Craftsmen, after ten years of apprenticeship, forged and tempered the steel blades in spiritual ceremonies. Many of these beliefs and traditions have survived and represent a significant element in Japanese culture today. Of all of the masters of sword making at the time, perhaps the greatest was Toshiru Yoshimitsu.

The Legend of Yoshimitsu's *Tantō*

After a dramatic battle, the Kurama temple had been destroyed, and the local community pooled resources for its reconstruction. Unlike other temples of the day, The Kurama temple complex did not have its own blacksmiths to forge the swords for their warrior monks. Therefore, errand boys were sent to Kyoto to retrieve building materials such as nails and saws.

One such boy travelled the perilous road from Kurama to Kyoto, searching for a smith. At last, he came across the distinguished Tōshirō Yoshimitsu. He asked the great sword maker to aid in the reconstruction, and Yoshimitsu obliged. In the following months, the errand boy faithfully delivered the nails and materials from Yoshimitsu's shop to the temple complex, narrowly escaping several dangers along the way.

As the seasons changed, the boy had raised enough courage to ask the great Yoshimitsu for one of his famous *tantō* daggers. He told him of the dangerous road he took every day, and promised that he would personally supply his shop with wood until the dagger was complete. Yoshimitsu agreed, and the boy kept his promise, bringing him daily wood through storms and snow.

After three years, the boy reminded Yoshimitsu of their deal. The swordsmith honored his arrangement, and finally finished a special *tantō* in exchange for all of the boy's service. Filled with joy, the boy showed the dagger to his friends and continued his work on the temple until it was completed.

Yet when it became widely known that the boy had a *tantō* created by the great Tōshirō Yoshimitsu, sinister forces grew envious. One day, when the errand boy was walking along the dangerous road, a terrible storm emerged. He took shelter under a cedar tree and fell asleep. A monstrous spider eyed the dagger, and also the boy for a feast. The spider trapped the boy in a web cocoon, yet before he was able to feed, the dagger magically unsheathed itself, woke the boy, cut the webs, and startled the spider away.

On the next day, the boy's travels were interrupted by a beautiful woman who flirtatiously entreated him for his *tantō*. When the boy refused to give up his prize, the woman transformed into a terrible spirit and reached for the dagger. The boy quickly used it and cut its hand, causing the spirit to flee away.

On the third day, the boy was met by a wealthy vassal making a pilgrimage to the temple. He asked the boy about the amazing knife, and the boy told him of his adventures with it. The vassal recognized the amazing blade for what it was, and offered the boy twice his annual salary for it. The boy agreed to sell it, and the vassal named it "The Spider Slasher." The boy happily lived with his wealth, while the *tantō* was passed down in the vassal's family for generations.

• • •

As students of swordsmanship, we can learn from "The Legend of Yoshimitsu's *Tantō*" that a great sword is well worth a high price, and that a worthy blade may take great sacrifice and hard work to attain. Likewise, a great swordsman does not become great overnight, but is forged through rigorous training and perilous experiences. Lastly, we see that a great sword can represent something more than a work of fine craftsmanship or a weapon of self-defense. Such a blade should be respected and kept in a place of honor.

Just ten years after grasping power, Minamoto Yoritomo died, and his wife (of the Hōjō clan, a surviving branch of the Taira clan) ruled in his stead. The title of Shogun passed from father to son, and each ruler would continue to hold heads of the Hōjō clan as regents, who arguably held more political influence than the Shogun.

Tired of wielding no real power, Emperor Go-Toba tried and failed in 1221 to overthrow the Shogun in the Jōkyū War. The imperial court was banished to Oki Island, but the Shogun would soon have greater problems. Creeping from the west was one of the most devastating military forces in the history of the world. Soon, Japan's martial prowess would be tested like never before.

For the last 68 years, the Mongol armies to the east had conquered the land surrounding Mongolia, and then exploded onto the continent with an unprecedented number of military victories, overtaking most of Asia. At the height of their empire, the Mongols seized over 24 million square kilometers of land, more than 16% of the earth's surface above water!

By 1274, Japan was in Kublai Khan's sights. The Mongol armies of 40,000 men and 900 ships invaded. They outnumbered the forces of the samurai (a mere 10,000) and wielded superior martial technology such as poison arrows and the cannon. It was a demoralizing blow to the noble followers of *bushido*. The Mongols fought without the codes of honor so familiar to the samurai. Age-old rules of war, discipline, and dignity were ignored by their enemies, yet the samurai stood their ground. On the day in which Mongol victory seemed imminent, a freakish storm bombarded the invading armies, forcing their retreat.

The proud Mongols had underestimated the land and warriors of Japan, and they were no doubt determined not to make the same mistake twice. A second invasion was launched upon the island nation in 1281 with a full-scale army of 140,000 men and a navy of 5,000 ships. The ensuing war strained the resources of the Shogun, severely injuring the regime's finances. Yet the outmatched samurai (40,000 strong) pressed back. For weeks, neither force gained or lost any ground, remaining at a stalemate near Kyushu. It was at that moment that the unthinkable happened. Powerful typhoons and storms again erupted from the sea, decimating the Mongol forces. The surviving invaders retreated, never again to threaten Japan.

The fateful storms that drove the Mongols back were known as "Divine Wind," a name that tragically would also be given to the Japanese suicide pilots of the Second World War—*Kamikaze*.

In the decades after the Mongol invasion, the Shogun's treasury failed to recover, leaving his regime vulnerable. When the time came to compensate the Lords and their samurai armies for their battles against the Mongols, the government came up short. It was only a matter of time before the outraged warriors would take what was rightfully theirs.

The surprise attack did not come from the ranks of the samurai but from the cloistered imperial court. Emperor Go-Daigo seized the opportunity to revolt against the shogunate and reinstate his family's reign. To meet the revolt, the current shogun called upon General Ashikaga Takauji. When the decisive battle came, Takauji's army marched out to meet the Emperor's forces, only to join them.

Takauji betrayed the Shogun, and helped Daigo rise with his disillusioned samurai armies. The Emperor initiated the "Kenmu Restoration" in 1334, with the goal to finally bring the imperial court out from its traditional supportive role. The promise of a new chapter in history was being written, but it was not to be.

Emperor Go-Daigo's first attempt had failed miserably, but it would not be his last. Before his rise, he had not yet convinced the majority of the land's mighty landowners to support him. He was not a samurai and did not have the loyalty of the battle-hardened warriors. Alas, he was betrayed and overthrown by his own trusted general, Takauji. A new line of shoguns had begun, and the government's capital was relocated to the city of Muromachi.

The mild stability of Takauji's rule would not go uncontested. Other great warlords, clan leaders, and powerful land owners plotted and schemed in the shadows. Usurpers sharpened their swords, and traditional allies secretly counted down the days to when they would betray one another. A new age of brutal conflict was on the horizon.

Tensions among the lords of the land were rising, yet one key ingredient was needed to spark the fire. 1,150 known Japanese sword makers at the time were busy at their trade, but none would become as well-known as the great Masamune. In 1328, Gorō Nyūdō Masamune, a brilliant swordsmith, developed and refined a new forging technique. It was a breakthrough that would create the most versatile and efficient weapon of pre-industrial Asia. His developments included a two-layer structure of a soft, flexible core and hard steel edge that gave much-improved cutting power and endurance. Masamune's "differential quenching" and the repeated doubling-over of steel billets (or "folding") revolutionized the industry. He had created the first modern *katana*.

The Legend of Masamune's River Test

Samurai, shoguns, emperors, and rulers from around the world (even in modern times) would learn of, and respect, the masterful works of Gorō Nyūdō Masamune. Several Masamune swords have been handed down through the ages, from father to son, and from leader to heir. Yet in his day, Masamune had rivals, and the question of who was truly the greatest sword maker would be contested from the battlefield to the monastery.

Legend has it that long ago, a young rival swordsmith by the name of Muramasa had challenged the much older Masamune to a competition. It was decided that they would both forge new swords and put them to the ultimate test. Their swords would not be tested by a warrior but rather by a slow flowing river. Only a passing by Buddhist monk was deemed impartial enough to judge which of the swords was truly superior.

When they had finished their secretive work, they produced two of the finest blades ever created. Muramasa named his sword "Juuchi Yosamu" (10,000 Cold Nights). He was the first to test his creation. He tied ropes to its hilt and suspended it over the water so that its cutting edge faced upstream. It was so sharp that as leaves floated down the water, they were split cleanly in two. Even fish and sticks would be divided by the force of the leisurely current.

Masamune complimented the boy on his fine work and brought his new sword, "Yawarakai-Te" (Tender Hands), to the test. It peacefully cut through the wind, and seemed to not even disturb the river. Interestingly, the fish and leaves always passed by one side of the blade or the other. Muramasa could not help but mock the old man. He chided him as the sword was retrieved, cleaned, and sheathed.

At last, the monk bowed to them both. He turned to Muramasa and congratulated him on the creation of such a fine sword. However, he declared that Masamune was the true winner of the contest. For Masamune's blade was not evil or bloodthirsty. It would not take an innocent life, nor would it cut needlessly. Therefore, it was truly the superior sword.

• • •

As students of swordsmanship, we learn from "The Legend of Masamune's River Test" that the greatest of warriors do not do anything in excess. In other words, no movement, nor action, is taken unless it is necessary. In a wider sense, we can see that violence should only be used when needed, and never against the innocent. Additionally, we see how foolish it can be to mock our elders, or misread our weaknesses as strengths.

The **Muromachi period** (1333–1568) began with a surge of power struggles and wars. Emperor Go-Daigo, still determined to rule, fled with those loyal to him to the southern city of Yoshino. The imperial family there created a "Southern Court," protected by the armies of those dedicated to the end of the shogunate. Meanwhile, the new Ashikaga Shogunate established the "Northern Court," guarded by an equally menacing coalition of armies. A civil war erupted between the North and the South, with each battle decided on the edge of the samurai's sword. As the struggle continued, several lords held back their samurai, content to observe the conflict from afar rather than get involved. Yet they too, in only a matter of time, would be forced into the chaos.

This conflict, along with many others springing up between clans, unraveled into the Sengoku period (or "Warring States" period), the bloody age in which the majority of samurai stories, books, and movies are set today. It is the era of the Ōnin War, in which even the historic city of Kyoto would be burned to the ground. The eastern Hosokawa clan and the western Yamana clan met in battle. Warrior monks entered the fray. As more and more *daimyōs* (lords) turned on their neighbors and scrambled for power, the nation broke into an increasing number of independent states, like so many shards of shattered glass.

Rival clans could not build armies quickly enough. The honorable and traditional samurai were in high demand, and the wages they were paid increased. Often, warriors arose out of the lower classes, and made a name for themselves as new samurai. In the political chaos, the early forms of *bushido* became even more important to the integrity of the samurai, and the nation, as a stabilizing code of ethics and standards. An example of the honorable adherence to *bushido* in battle comes from the story of Uesugi Kenshin, a great samurai general.

The Legend of the Rival's Salt

In the fourth battle of Kawanakajima in the year 1561, Uesugi Kenshin again faced his greatest and fiercest rival, Takeda Shingen. Although their armies fought relentlessly and they had faced each other in near fatal duels, they had a tremendous respect for one another. Over the years, they had come to recognize each other's skill, and admired each other's resolve. Perhaps, under different circumstances, Kenshin and Shingen may have been friends. However, in their day, their clans were sworn enemies, and the future of the nation was in the balance.

On the eve of their most epic battle, Kenshin learned that the supplies to Shingen's forces had been cut off. He knew at once that they must have been starving, even as he was asked what to do with the information. Rather than face an opponent on unequal footing, Kenshin ordered his samurai to hold back. He immediately had food and salt sent over to his enemies' forces, ensuring that Shingen's men would live through the night and face him the following morning in full strength. The next day, the swords of the two relentless armies clashed and sparked as they had so many times before.

Years later, Takeda Shingen led his clan against the forces of other legendary samurai such as Tokugawa Ieyasu, claiming victories large and small. Yet after a mighty battle, he returned to his tent and at long last succumbed to an old injury. News of his great rival's death quickly reached Kenshin. When he heard of it, he wept openly. He turned to his armies and publicly declared the event a tragedy, as the land had lost one of its greatest heroes.

· · ·

As students of swordsmanship, we can learn from "The Legend of the Rival's Salt" that credit should be given where it is due, and even those who oppose and challenge us the most can still be deserving of our deepest respect. Most importantly, we can see that even when one is faced with the savagery of war, the core principles of *bushido* can still be honored.

Samurai are commonly seen today as the archetypal honorable warrior. Even in the eyes of the warlords of the Sengoku period, their codes and skills were highly valued. Yet some lords looked greedily for another option. As neither the Shogun nor the Emperor could maintain order, every lord was forced to fend for himself. The services of a less noble warrior, one that could sneak into a rival's home and strike or poison them in the shadows, were also required. This stealthy assassin would become known as the *Ninja*.

Interestingly, it was in this chaotic Muromachi period that many of the iconic traditional Japanese art forms really flourished. These forms include the tea ceremony, rock gardens, flower arranging, theater, calligraphy, and painting. In the meantime, trade with China and Korea was also booming. Japan's 3,550 swordsmiths were also in their heyday, supplying the various civil wars with their martial works of art.

By 1542, the relative solitary nature of the Japanese archipelago changed forever. Portuguese traders and Jesuit missionaries arrived in Kyushu, bringing with them trade goods and Christianity, which were mostly welcomed by the western warlords. In their journals, the missionaries expressed their fascination with the Japanese people and their sophisticated and complex culture. As *daimyōs* converted to Christianity, they often pressured their subjects to do the same. Yet these warlords may have been most interested in a new tactical advantage imported by the foreigners—muskets.

In an age shaped by armies who won battles by breaking off into several one-on-one duels, guns would change everything. No longer must a man be highly skilled and disciplined to defeat a foe. With a gun in hand, even a coward with almost no training could now prevail in battle. Across Japan, once-legendary sword craftsmen were ordered to convert their hallowed shops into crude firearm factories. The military advantages of muskets would transform Japanese warfare forever, and herald the end of Japan's medieval times.

Early Modern Japan

The heir to the Ashikaga Shogunate was assassinated. It happened in the city of Muromachi in 1565. Left in the wake of the assassination, there was a critical vacuum of power that would take nearly a decade to fill. The resulting battles were the ultimate contest of supremacy. On their own, each clan was powerless to bring an end to the fighting. Yet, as brilliant samurai generals arose, several clans unified behind them. In the end, three men would prove to have what it took to shape the future of their nation, by the edge of their blades and by the smoke of their rifles. In time, these three men would come to be known as Japan's "Three Unifiers."

With Japan still divided in the later years of the Sengoku period, historians lack a single capital city by which to name the era following the Muromachi period. Two major castles, each held by the most powerful warlords of the age, are thus conventionally combined. The **Azuchi–Momoyama period** (1573–1600) would see the end of Japan's countless civil wars and the rise of a unified nation.

The first of Japan's three unifiers was the unconventional and innovative Oda Nobunaga. He was a powerful *daimyō* of the Oda clan. As a young man, he was thought of as brash, boisterous, unruly, and ruthless. Yet Oda Nobunaga soon made a name for himself for thinking outside the box. United clans and territories thrived under his command. He is known for dramatically reforming and improving Japan's economic systems and brilliantly implementing a new system of warfare that capitalized on the combination of firearms, castles, and never-before-seen strategies. For example, in the Battle of Okehazama, he set up dummy soldiers, filled with straw and dressed in spare armor, to misdirect enemy forces away from the stronghold they were tasked to protect.

Although the maverick Oda Nobunaga provided the first signs of the end of the Warring States period, it would be the second unifier,

Toyotomi Hideyoshi, and the final unifier, Tokugawa Ieyasu, that would ultimately bring the territories of the land under one flag. Japan's unification, and the three leaders seen as its facilitators, can be compared to a meal of rice. It is said that Nobunaga prepared the rice, Hideyoshi cooked the rice, and Ieyasu ate the rice. Their roles are commonly seen as practical consequences to their three dramatically different personalities and strategies. These differences can be represented in "The Legend of the Songbird."

The Legend of the Songbird

Japan's three unifiers met as friends one day to drink tea. As they enjoyed each other's company they were joined by a cuckoo bird. The three all wanted the bird to sing, but it remained silent.

Oda Nobunaga threatened the bird. "If you don't sing," he said, "then I will kill you."

Toyotomi Hideyoshi stopped Nobunaga and shook his head. "If you don't sing," he told the bird, "then I will make you sing."

At last, Tokugawa Ieyasu held Hideyoshi back and addressed the bird, "If you don't sing, I will wait for you to sing."

When the cuckoo bird finally made a beautiful sound, only Ieyasu remained to enjoy it.

• • •

As students of swordsmanship, we learn from the "Legend of the Songbird" that the greatest of warriors do not force victory (cheat), or negotiate victory (claim a win from an unclear situation). Rather, one ought to allow victory to unfold and emerge in battle, to the one who is most deserving. An honorable duelist will accept the results of any duel, with neither complaint nor boasting.

Oda Nobunaga unified about half of the clans of Japan with his rule while at Azuchi Castle. Rather than recognize his lords based upon how much land they owned, he sorted them based upon their rice production. To add to his unorthodox methods, he allied himself with Christian groups, encouraging them to revolt against his enemies, who were primarily Buddhist. Before the Siege of Inabayama Castle, Nobunaga weakened his enemy's forces by convincing several of the lords to abandon their leaders, who he had portrayed as weak and foolish.

In several battles, Nobunaga proved his ruthlessness and spread horror by indiscriminately cutting down countless victims. In the Third Siege of Nagashima, for example, after having lost the majority of his armies trying to overtake the fortress, Nobunaga surrounded the building with a wall, and set the fortress on fire.

Rather than promote generals based on their social class or family history, Nobunaga looked to a warrior's skill and talent. In fact, one of his greatest generals, Toyotomi Hideyoshi, was born of a peasant family, but would prove his prowess in battle. He served Nobunaga well, and would become the second of the Three Unifiers.

In 1582, one of Nobunaga's own officers turned on him and killed him. Many turned on the officer to avenge their lord, but it was Toyotomi Hideyoshi who cut him down and inherited Nobunaga's legacy.

In battle, Toyotomi Hideyoshi often claimed victory by acting quickly and decisively. Under his rule, Japan entered into a new era of harsher governance. To him, unification was paramount. Therefore, the possibility of rebellion had to be crushed. Christians were oppressed, persecuted, and even crucified. Hideyoshi even quelled a slave rebellion by reclassifying the lowest of Japan's classes in a way that freed most of Japan's slaves. He introduced strict class laws that would remain in effect for the next 300 years. Travel between cities was highly restricted and regulated. Hideyoshi would also build several temples and Osaka

Castle, the largest and most impressive of Japan's fortifications of the day.

During this period, samurai (about 10% of the population) became the "two-sword man," wearing both a short and a long sword as a mark of their privilege. It was an effective statement, because swords were quickly becoming illegal. No one, except for the established warriors, was allowed by Hideyoshi to keep their swords. In fact, laws were created that would completely prohibit peasants from becoming samurai.

Even as they enjoyed their new status, the samurai themselves could sense that their quality of life was on the decline. Up to this point, they had traditionally made their living on a fixed stipend from landowners. Yet now, many had no choice but to become bureaucrats or take up some type of trade. As the material well-being of many samurai declined, several felt frustrated by their inability to improve their situation.

Hideyoshi facilitated the unification of even more clans in Japan, yet he knew that he had to do something with the vast armies of samurai in peacetime. For generations they participated in endless civil wars. Standing armies, known for shifting loyalties, were a threat to Japan's stability. He therefore decided that he would conquer China.

Over several years, Hideyoshi kept in contact with the Koreans, requesting passage through their lands in order to invade China. However, time after time, the Koreans refused. At last, he declared war against Korea. This was a terribly unpopular decision and would lead in the future to several *daimyōs* pulling their support from a Toyotomi shogunate. In his second failed attempt to conquer the Korean peninsula, he was killed in battle. In order to maintain morale, most of his troops would not learn of his fall until after their retreat back into Japan.

Who was Hideyoshi's rightful successor? In a further attempt to quash rebellion or civil war, Hideyoshi had set a contingency plan among his most trusted allies, generals, and friends, known as the "Council of Five Regents." He had planned for his son to become the next shogun and had each member of the council swear oaths to protect and preserve his son, Toyotomi Hideyori, until he was old enough to become the heir of the shogunate.

There were two problems with this plan. First, Hideyoshi died in 1593, far earlier than expected, leaving his son fatherless at the age of five. As a five-year-old garners little loyalty from armies on his own, a tremendous amount of trust was placed with the Council of Five Regents. This led to the second problem. One of the five regents had been planning for years to seize control for himself when the time was right. And now, the time was right. This trusted ally of Hideyoshi? It was none other than the third of the Unifiers—Tokugawa Ieyasu.

The Legend of Tokugawa Ieyasu

Born to teenage parents (a *daimyo* and a samurai) and half-brother to 11 siblings, Tokugawa Ieyasu (originally named Matsudaira Takechiyo) was raised among the elite classes of Japan. However, his early childhood was spent amid countless battles and civil war. His family, the Matsudaira clan, was split with one half supporting one powerful clan (the Imagawa), and the second supporting another (the Oda). Some family members were killed in the dispute, and he was sent off at age five, as a hostage, by his father in exchange for troop support from the Imagawa clan.

As Ieyasu was en route to the Imagawa clan, he was abducted by the Oda. For months, the leaders of the Oda clan threatened Ieyasu's father, ordering him to join them, or else they would destroy his son. His father refused, declaring that such a loss would only show his dedication to his cause. Alas, Ieyasu's father was killed by his own allies after they had been bribed by the Oda clan.

The senselessness of the constant betrayals and conflicts was not lost on young Ieyasu. After all, His life was put in danger several times before his 10th birthday. Yet rather than allow the chaos to fill him with rage, he became a contemplative young man, quiet, and above all else, patient.

The Imagawa clan retaliated and captured the eldest son and heir to the Oda family leadership. A deal was made to exchange hostages, and thus everything worked out so that Ieyasu could live with the Imagawa in Sunpu as his father had intended. (Sunpu became an important city to Ieyasu, and he'd often return to it later in life.)

At this time, a "hostage" was considered less like a prisoner, and more like an adopted son. Under Imagawa Yoshimoto, the head of the clan, Ieyasu was raised with all the education, comforts, and accommodations that he would have expected from his own parents. He was taught calligraphy and poetry. He mastered the arts of swordsmanship and studied the great samurai of the past. Ieyasu was fascinated with the precepts of the honor codes of the samurai, and often wondered if such strict self-discipline could be translated into a form of government, another subject of his studies. Perhaps it was at this time, at age 13, that he secretly determined to one day unite the clans and bring lasting peace to Japan.

In 1558, Ieyasu's mettle as a warrior would first be tested in the Siege of Terabe Castle, and again in the Siege of Odaka, leading to his first victories. While he spent the night at Odaka, his lord, Imagawa Yoshimoto, was killed in the Battle of Okehazama against a new brilliant strategist, Oda Nobunaga, who had utilized straw-filled decoys in his victory.

Ieyasu had been a hostage to Yoshimoto. Yet with his death, he was without a master, and became a kind of *ronin*. A crucial decision had to be made. Would he continue to fight for the Imagawa clan? After all, it is with them that his wife and child lived. Would he follow the majority of his family in support of the Oda clan? With the new strict laws preventing a samurai from becoming a farmer or merchant, his options were few. If he desired to rule over the nation, then he must continue with his military career. He developed a strategy, an answer to save his family and his nation, and one that would take a lifetime to come to fruition. It is this kind of contemplation and careful strategizing, paired with his courage, patience, and vigilance that would come to define Ieyasu's life.

In 1561, Ieyasu sought out the unconventional leader who was uniting several clans behind him—Oda Nobunaga. He rallied forces by declaring his new allegiance and promptly captured the fortress of Kaminogō. He kept the fortresses' occupants alive and made a deal for a hostage swap that the Imagawa clan could not refuse—a castle filled with people, in exchange for his wife and child. Years later, to further show his allegiance to the powerful Nobunaga, Ieyasu insisted that his son marry Nobunaga's daughter.

His reputation as a cool-minded general grew, thanks to the stories shared among his men with other samurai. One such story took place after he had led his army to a narrow bridge over a raging river that they needed to cross. The flow was intense, and Ieyasu's horse was becoming agitated. The warriors watched with curiosity. What would the great Ieyasu do? It was said that his horsemanship skills rivaled even those of the legendary Tomoe Gozen. To their surprise, he didn't charge through or force his horse across the bridge. Rather, Ieyasu dismounted and slowly led the animal, carefully, across the bridge. On the battlefield, on the road, and on Ieyasu's many hawking trips, the horse had proven its loyalty, and was thus treated with gratitude and respect. Despite his callous strategies, the stories of Ieyasu often speak of a certain compassion, seen most in how he treated his allies, friends, and even old enemies who had sworn loyalty to him.

In many of the battles before him, Ieyasu was careful to remember which warlords, vassals, and samurai were most loyal. He rewarded them greatly with land, castles, and servants. He also studied the histories of the betrayals and rivalries of the clans with which he allied and fought. This information proved useful to him as he rallied more forces to Oda Nobunaga's cause, sometimes betraying others just before they betrayed him.

While the samurai rule was slowly turning toward an era of peace, there were many who resented the powerful warriors, namely the Monto warring monks, now required to pay high taxes. In the fight against rebelling monks in the Battle of Azukizaka, Ieyasu led an army with similar monks who were loyal to Nobunaga. The strategy was both practical and psychological. Ieyasu led from the front lines, taking bullets to his armor in the process. He personally dueled with any dissenting warriors, and inspired loyalty among his supporters and among many of those he captured.

With Oda Nobunaga, Ieyasu captured Kyoto in 1568. They also worked together to successfully subdue the rival Azai and Asakura clans in the Battle of Anegawa. It was in that battle that Nobunaga's friend and retainer, Toyotomi Hideyoshi, would first lead his own troops. Several brave Asakura clan samurai covered the retreat of their forces but were no match for Nobunaga's riflemen.

With his growing number of military successes, Ieyasu decided to put his old family name behind him and redefine himself with a new identity. He petitioned the emperor to allow him to change his surname to Tokugawa. It was an interesting choice, as it would imply that he was descended from the Minamoto clan (The same clan as the legendary tragic hero, Minamoto Yoshitsune.) The emperor approved, and it is by this name that he is mostly known today.

Although he constantly, and bravely, supported his lord, Ieyasu never lost sight of growing his own powerful influence. He returned to the warring clans of his childhood, and decided to join forces with the Takeda clan to completely capture the remaining territories of the Imagawa, including his favorite city of Sunpu. Yet he decided at this point to set the city of Hamamatsu as the temporary capital for his territories.

Once he had met his own goals, he quickly turned on the Takeda, and allied with their sworn enemies, creating an overpowering force against them. The Takeda responded by joining forces with the Hōjō clan and attacked Ieyasu's lands, overwhelming his samurai. At the Battle of Mikatagahara, Nobunaga would send to his loyal supporter several troops, but they would not be enough. Ieyasu considered his options, listened to the advice from his generals, and retreated.

Ieyasu was determined to be dignified and honorable in his loss. After all, it was his betrayal of the Takeda that led to the heavy casualties his forces had sustained. As he retreated to the nearest stronghold, he ordered that his defeated warriors be welcomed back into the nearest fortification with drums, blazing torches, and proper ceremony. As the Takeda armies looked on, they were confused by the pageantry, and suspected that the calculating Ieyasu was up to something. They resorted to wait out the night in order to avoid some sort of trap. There is no doubt that the defeated Ieyasu was perplexed by this response, and promptly ordered his elite band of ninjas to attack the sleeping Takeda. The plan worked out flawlessly, disorienting the Takeda and forcing their retreat. In the coming years, the combined armies of Ieyasu and Nobunaga would continue to push the Takeda back and claim their lands, the Kai Province.

Yet the ruthless Nobunaga was not blind to Ieyasu's rise in power. When he heard of a rumor from his daughter that her detested mother-in-law (Ieyasu's wife) was planning to betray Nobunaga, he brought the allegation to Ieyasu. It was the ultimate test of loyalty and one that would change the history of Japan. If Ieyasu believed Nobunaga, he would lose his wife and the heir to his legacy. If he defended his son and wife, he could be labeled as a traitor and threat to Nobunaga. Another civil war would ensue, and the nation would be plunged into another age of endless fighting. If Ieyasu was not committed to his lifelong plan to rule a united Japan, this would be his last chance to turn back.

Ieyasu ordered for his wife and eldest son to be put to death honorably. It was a decision that would torture Ieyasu for the rest of his life. Oda Nobunaga, consequently, never questioned his loyalty again.

Ieyasu's plan could not afford another look into his true intentions. Therefore, he named his third son as his heir. It was a strategic move, because the boy had been adopted by the most powerful *daimyō* at the time, a favored general of Nobunaga—Toyotomi Hideyoshi. In 1582, Nobunaga was assassinated. Ieyasu immediately led his samurai to battle against the assassins, but Hideyoshi had beat him to it.

Nobunaga's death had come too quickly, and Ieyasu was not yet ready to claim the title of Shogun. Although his forces were substantial and his territories great, he was not seen as the obvious choice in the eyes of most of the *daimyōs*. The lands and the armies of Nobunaga were preyed upon by the most powerful warlords of the day, each making themselves obvious targets and rivals to each other. Others were more strategic. For example, one of Ieyasu's aides was killed in the Kai province, so Ieyasu quickly moved his forces into the region and claimed it for himself under justifiable pretenses. The Hōjō clan grew suspicious of Ieyasu, but he made a deal with them. They accepted Ieyasu's offer of a portion of his land to them, preventing several battles.

Shibata Katsuie had risen up as a rival to Hideyoshi's dominance. As with most of the other battles and power struggles of the time, Ieyasu held back, studying the shifting power dynamics, rather than get involved. When Hideyoshi proved victorious, Ieyasu sensed that Hideyoshi would soon become too powerful. In a clever move to gain support, Ieyasu allied his forces with those of Oda Nobukatsu, the oldest surviving son of Oda Nobunaga, and fortified the major Oda castle of Owari.

Several battles, starting at Owari (known as "The Komaki Campaign"), took place as Hideyoshi moved to counter the growing resistance to his dominance. Ieyasu had gambled nearly everything against this victory, but it still had not come. Likewise, Hideyoshi matched each defensive strategy until the days and months dragged into a stalemate. Ieyasu could not allow Hideyoshi's armies to triumph, or else his dream would die with his armies.

At last, Hideyoshi and Nobukatsu negotiated a truce. Ieyasu contemplated the ramifications of this and immediately supported it, sending his second son to be an adopted son of Hideyoshi as a sign of his compliance. Thus began an uneasy new alliance between Hideyoshi and Ieyasu, one that would grow stronger over time.

By 1590, there was only one remaining independent *daimyō* who was not allied with Hideyoshi. It was the leader of the Hōjō clan, rulers over the Kanto region for over 100 years. Numerous battles and sieges were carried out with the combined forces of Hideyoshi and Ieyasu against the Hōjō. Hideyoshi was victorious, but still eyed Ieyasu's own five provinces and capital city of Hamamatsu. Perhaps he thought that the peoples of the regions were too loyal to Ieyasu. It may be that he thought Ieyasu may stage a revolt from those territories. Whatever his reasoning, Hideyoshi offered Ieyasu the eight provinces of the Kanto region in exchange for his five.

If this was a test of his loyalty, Ieyasu passed it. He agreed to the deal and relocated to a small and obscure fishing village in the Kanto region—Edo.

No longer surrounded by his faithful subjects, Ieyasu now had to rise in favor among the people he had just defeated in costly battles. He turned the challenge into an opportunity and proved to be a capable and effective leader of the region. In Edo, he built a massive five-story castle like nothing else before it. Local economics were improved, the Hōjō were supportive of him, and he was able to garner tremendous support with, now, a second major region of the nation. Ieyasu had thus become the second most powerful *daimyō* in Japan.

Still, Ieyasu waited. The time was not yet right for his ultimate rise to power. Hideyoshi had met often with the Emperor, requesting the title of Shogun over all of Japan. He invited the Emperor to plays and concerts. With gifts and letters, he tried to impress him, but the Emperor would ultimately refuse his requests. On the other hand, the Emperor found much in common with Ieyasu, and was pleased with the marriage of his son with Ieyasu's granddaughter.

In his old age, Hideyoshi became more cruel and unpredictable. He still did not have an heir, and he knew all the work he had done to unite Japan could be undone without one. He decided to adopt a son and name him his heir. Yet not too long after, at age 60, he would father a son. To prevent any internal conflict, he had his adopted son killed, along with his entire family, and buried them in the "Tomb of the Traitors."

It was then, in 1598, that Hideyoshi called upon the Council of Five Elders, his closest friends and allies, and ordered them to rule in his stead as regents and to protect his infant son, Toyotomi Hideyori. They were to watch over him until he was old enough to take his place as the rightful ruler of Japan. Ieyasu, by far the most popular and powerful of the five, swore with the others to protect the boy and do as their lord desired.

When Hideyoshi launched his campaigns against Korea in 1592, Ieyasu was careful to listen to the general opinion of the *daimyōs* at the time. Hideyoshi was growing ill, and his new war was not at all popular. Therefore, Ieyasu and the Tokugawa clan stayed in his Kanto territories, far away from the conflict, strengthening his fortifications and relations.

At last, Hideyoshi died in battle. The time had finally come for Ieyasu. The years of servitude under Imagawa Yoshimoto, Oda Nobunaga, and Toyotomi Hideyoshi had come to this. All he had done to prove his loyalty, including turning on friends and sentencing his own wife and son to death, and all of his careful strategizing and patience, had come to this moment.

Ieyasu acted quickly. He made alliances with all of Hideyoshi's enemies (forming the "Eastern Army") and captured several key fortifications. By now, one of the five elders had died of old age, leading the remaining three to oppose Ieyasu. They were outraged at Ieyasu for his aggressive behavior, and rallied the forces loyal to Hideyoshi against him (forming the "Western Army").

Several battles and shifting alliances over the next two years between the Eastern and Western factions of Japan led to what is possibly the most important and decisive battle in all of Japanese history—the Battle of Sekigahara. It took place on October 21, 1600 and would be fought by over 160,000 samurai.

The day was haunted by thick fog. Raging storms gave way to an eerie quiet. The armies slowly moved toward each other. It was only when the fog lifted that they realized they were already within striking distance of each other! In the mud and rain, the Eastern Army fought against the much larger Western Army with swords clashing and guns firing. A large part of the Western Army had secretly allied with Ieyasu months before and remained neutral in the conflict. This caused disorder and panic to fill many factions of the Western Army, leading some key generals to switch their allegiance to Ieyasu, while others retreated. As the brutal conflict drew on, more and more defectors joined the Eastern Army, finally leading to their complete and absolute victory.

Many years later, in order to ensure that there would be no contest to his rule, Ieyasu launched an attack against Osaka Castle, the late Hideyoshi's most powerful stronghold, where the young Toyotomi Hideyori (now a man) was being kept. The siege was costly, with thousands of Hideyori's *rōnin* as well as Ieyasu's samurai falling in battle. At last, Ieyasu sent a lady samurai to deliver a message to Hideyori's mother. It was a call for a truce and an end to the conflict. As the truce was being signed, Ieyasu's men quickly filled in Osaka Castle's moat with sand. Before Hideyori's protectors knew what was happening, Ieyasu stormed the castle, betraying the truce, and burned it to the ground.

Ieyasu had at last triumphed over the warring clans of his day. He showered those who had been loyal to him with land and rewards, giving them a higher status in society over those who had fought against him. In 1603, the emperor officially recognized Ieyasu as the true Shogun and leader of Japan. Thus Ieyasu secured his reign. Just two years later, he retired to the city of Sunpu and left the title of Shogun to his son, ensuring a peaceful transition of power upon his own death. His family, the Tokugawa Shogunate, would rule the entire Japanese archipelago for over 250 years.

Was Ieyasu a hero or a villain? The answer may not be clear. While he exemplified many traits of an honorable follower of *bushido*, he is also guilty of many of the same cruelties and horrors forced upon the people of Japan by his predecessors. He finally unified Japan and ushered in an era of peace, but at a terrible cost and with strict laws limiting many freedoms previously enjoyed by Japan's citizens. It is clear, however, that his strategy was carefully calculated, and that his tactics proved effective, placing him among the greatest of Japan's leaders, and among the fiercest of samurai.

• • •

As students of swordsmanship, we can learn a great deal from the "Legend of Tokugawa Ieyasu." First, is that he had a clear objective, known only to himself. However, he understood his options and was willing to adjust his plan when needed. In a duel, you must have a target in your mind, but you must equally be aware of the costs and benefits to each action. Be aware of the body language of your opponent, and take no small hint for granted. A decisive attack may leave you vulnerable, while an emphasis on defense may lead to missing a key opportunity. Similarly, a great duelist must never become overconfident. A careful assessment of your strengths and weaknesses, compared to your opponent, should be kept in mind. If your advantage is clear, keep it secret. If your opponent sees you as the weaker fighter, use that to your advantage. A great duelist is willing to sacrifice a small opportunity in order to take advantage of a greater one later in the duel. Lastly, a great duelist remembers that sword fighting is a deeply mental sport and will use psychological methods (such as strong vocalizations or facial expression) when advantageous.

The establishment of the Tokugawa Shogunate, ruling from the city of Edo, issued in the peaceful **Edo period** (1600–1868). Massive construction projects took shape, infrastructure improved, and it wasn't long before the capital became one of the largest cities in the world.

With military control in hand, the Shogun moved to gain greater political and economic control. By 1615, Tokugawa Ieyasu had gathered the 260 *daimyōs* of the nation together and read to them new strict policies that all lords and samurai were to follow—the *Buke Shohatto* (Laws for the Military Houses). It was thereafter law, enforced by his son, that the *daimyōs* must (among other things): serve the Shogun in person (every other year); never be social with commoners, samurai, or lords from other domains; maintain law and order within their domains; and report any conspiracies, inter-domain marriages, and even repairs made to their castles, directly to the shogunate.

The *buke shohatto* also introduced new laws regulating the lifestyle of the Samurai. Rather than send all of the nation's warriors off to battle neighboring countries, the Tokugawa Shogunate decided to disband their several armies (creating over 500,000 *rōnin*) and redefine what it meant to be a samurai. For example, all members of the elite warrior class were required to spend their time pursuing the hobbies of the aristocracy, such as archery, swordsmanship, horsemanship, poetry, calligraphy, and classical literature. They were to become literate and cultured. Samurai were also to live with modest pay and exercise frugality. *Bushido* was finally standardized in its modern form, with a heavy Confucian influence. Confucianism, by now, had eclipsed Zen Buddhism as the most popular philosophy of the warrior class.

Born of *rōnin* parents into this era of the evolving identity of the samurai was Daidōji Yūzan. He studied military science in Edo from masters who directly served Tokugawa Ieyasu. He would continue on to serve as a samurai for a couple of clan leaders but was most perplexed with a wide-spread problem. Without the threat of battle, many young samurai were living shamefully, oblivious to the rich cultural heritage and responsibilities they had inherited. They had grown lazy, selfish, and unruly. Therefore, he studied *bushido*, learned from the great samurai of his age and from the past, and wrote the definitive guide on the subject—*Budō Shoshin-shū* (The Warrior's Primer). It was widely circulated at the time, and continues to inform students of the tenets of *bushido* today.

They may have had a guide on how to live, but what were the wandering *rōnin* and the redefined samurai to do? Although sword training, based upon the ancient ways of kenjutsu, was mandated by the shogunate, there were no battles to fight. It was in this age that non-lethal duels and spars were practiced among the *rōnin* as well as the samurai class. Rather than use their metal swords, wooden or bamboo swords were created. War veterans, along with monks, became masters of the new (yet ancient) martial art. Strict rules were put in place, along with a point system to determine a winner. But was it a sport? No, it was a sincere exercise in the traditional ways of the samurai and the code of *bushido*. It was a method of swordsmanship training in peacetime, coupled with character growth and a strengthening of the mind and spirit. It would become known as "Kendo."

By now, the Tokugawa Shogunate had set a trend for itself. The Shogun gained complete control over the country and its culture. Throughout the Edo period, numerous laws and decrees would be made that further regulated the everyday life of every citizen of the country. Obedience, and knowing one's place in society, was paramount. With such strict laws, peace and order were maintained, but the individual freedom of each citizen was severely limited. Even the clothing one was to wear was highly regulated. Women were required to stay in the home and only travel when in possession of special authorizations and paperwork. Farmers were not allowed to eat from the rice they grew. Penalties for even minor offenses were harsh, including death by boiling. Great efforts were also made to free the country from outside influence. Trade, travel, and contact with the outside world (especially Europe) were cut off. Japan would remain isolated for the next 200 years.

During this time, Christians were especially heavily oppressed. Their meetings were outlawed, their missionaries expelled, and their leaders were often sent to fiery executions. Small pockets of Christian rebellions grew in response to the strict taxes and religious persecution, culminating in the Shimabara Rebellion of 1638, in which Christian peasants defended Hara castle against the Shogun's forces for four months. Alas, the rebels were defeated, and their religion was completely outlawed.

The population of Japan doubled. New cities sprang up along the improved road systems built for the elaborate processions *daimyōs* would lead from their lands to the capital and back. The wealthy leaders were entertained by new puppet theatres and *Geishas*. One of the rare imports allowed from Europe, Dutch books (especially science books), sparked an intellectual revolution in Japan. Literacy rates increased, countless books were published and schools raised, laying an educational foundation that would directly benefit Japan's economy for generations to come.

In the streets, many samurai and *rōnin* competed with one another to determine the superior swordsmen. Several schools of kendo and kenjutsu sprang up, each claiming to give their students the greater advantage. Yet for one young student, these claims were not enough. He demanded a scientific approach be taken to find exactly how best to defeat not just one foe, but several at a time. This boy was Miyamoto Musashi.

The Legend of Musashi's Duel

Orphaned by age seven, Miyamoto Musashi was raised by his uncle, a Buddhist priest. He was a solitary, awkward boy. His hair and appearance was often unkempt, and he was prone to obsess over things he didn't fully understand. Swordsmanship grasped his attention, but he found the many schools around him to be sloppy and unreliable. Although the school masters had big claims, Musashi determined to put each technique and teaching to the test, to truly determine what was most effective in a duel. He would soon be known as the first in Japan to revolutionize sword fighting instruction by boiling it down to a science!

When asked about his studies, he answered confidently about his skills. He'd often desire to test new techniques out on opponents, and many would oblige (perhaps in part because they wanted to whittle away at the surprising confidence of such a young boy). At age 13, he was challenged to a duel to the death against an experienced swordsman... and won.

He traded his steel *katana* for a *bokutō* (wooden sword), and would sometimes duel using two. By age 16, he had defeated an accomplished samurai and then left to travel on foot as an ascetic *rōnin*, dedicating his life to finding more opponents and perfecting his own technique. He'd casually defeat or best one opponent after another, soon becoming a legend. By age 28, he had survived 60 deadly duels, by far the greatest record of his day.

Of course, his success and his claim to have found a style better than that taught in any school earned him rivals. The greatest of his rivals was the towering and fierce Sasaki Kojirō. Kojirō was the head of a prominent fencing school, a famous warrior, and an intimidating duelist. It was said that his stare was like piercing fire and his rapid movements like those of a swallow. He challenged Musashi to a duel to the death on a small sandbar in southern Japan. Musashi accepted, much to the horror of his associates.

When the time for the match had come, Kojirō had arrived, along with an eager crowd, standing menacingly on the edge of the ocean. He waited, with no sign of the young Musashi.

Alas, Musashi had overslept that morning. He stumbled from his bed, took only some water for his breakfast, and got on a boat to the sandbar. He did not bring a sword with him, so he casually took out his knife, whittled a wooden sword out of a spare oar, and fell back asleep.

When the combatants met, Kojirō insulted his rival for showing up late, looking so haggard, and for bringing such a pitiful-looking weapon. The duelists assumed their starting positions and stood stone-still for several minutes. The onlookers who had gathered were confused that two such powerful swordsmen would just be standing and staring at each other for so long.

Without warning, Kojirō quickly swung his sword down at Musashi's head, who also leapt forward with his makeshift *bokutō* with a great cry. The ribbon of Musashi's head had been cut in two and was taken away by the wind, revealing no wound. On the other hand, Kojirō was dealt a fatal blow to the head, and he collapsed in defeat. Musashi bowed to the crowd and returned to his boat.

The entire encounter was a test of Musashi's tactics. His last-minute *bokutō* was used to counter Kojirō's unusually long sword. His attire gave him a psychological advantage, and even his lateness allowed for the sun's position in the sky to go to his benefit. His overall technical and straightforward thinking would show later in his writings.

With this definitive duel, Musashi discontinued his quest to duel ever more partners,and moved on to life to live a life as the quintessential samurai. He created his own school, served as a soldier, and became highly skilled in several art forms. In his old age, Musashi wrote the book that would become the ultimate strategy guide for Japanese warriors and a staple of all Kendo libraries to this day—*The Book of Five Rings*.

• • •

As students of swordsmanship, we can learn a great deal from the "Legend of Miyamoto Musashi." First, he assumed nothing. He made his decisions based upon the best evidence he could find, and if no such evidence was available, he made no assumptions. Likewise, in a duel, if we pretend to know something about our opponent before we have good reason, we are setting ourselves up for failure. Second, we should not judge our skill based upon the flashiness or complexity of our techniques. Effectiveness, more than all else, is what is most important. Lastly, the value of practice and experience cannot be overstated. Sincere students of swordsmanship must practice, spar, and duel often in order to fully understand each technique and commit it to muscle memory.

By the late Edo period, the strict laws of the shogunate had taken their toll. Harsh taxes had left many farmers impoverished and disenfranchised. Corruption had run rampant among the shogunate and the *daimyōs*, whose public pursuits of pleasure and excess were not lost on the masses. Even the small stipend paid to the nation's samurai was cut, creating armies of even more *rōnin* overnight. The nation's issues multiplied exponentially in 1833 with flooding, severe cold weather, the four-year-long Tenpō famine, the Kōgo Fire of Edo, and a devastating earthquake. The majority of the nation's *daimyōs* weathered these disasters well, and many refused to provide any relief to the starving residents of their cities. Finally, in 1837, a merchant ship from the United States (bringing seven shipwrecked Japanese sailors home), was fired upon by the shogunate and driven away, an act the Americans would not forget.

In 1853, a fleet of massive war ships from the United Sates returned to the shores of Japan. The military show of force overwhelmed the Tokugawa Shogunate, and an agreement to open the country to travel and trade with the US, Great Britain, Russia, and other Western countries was made.

Noble samurai (such as Inoue Kaoru, Ito Hirobumi and Yamagata Aritomo) from the regions of Satsuma, Chōshū, and Tosa, along with disenfranchised citizens and *rōnin*, demanded that the Shogun immediately resign. But who would succeed the Shogun,

Tokugawa Yoshinobu, the 15th ruler of the Tokugawa line? The rebels already knew their answer. Quickly spreading was their philosophy of "Sonnō Jōi," in which they called for the expulsion of the barbaric shoguns and the restoration of the rightful ruler of Japan, the Emperor.

On November 9, 1867, hoping for a peaceful resolution to the conflict, the Shogun presented his resignation to the 122nd emperor of Japan, Emperor Meiji, and stepped down ten days later. However, many in the new imperial army called for the obliteration of the Tokugawa clan, marking the beginning of the Boshin War. This led to the ex-Shogun, Yoshinobu, to lead forces to capture the imperial court in Kyoto. To his surprise, the smaller yet modernized imperial army pushed him back. The Tokugawa fled to the north, establishing an independent and democratic country called the "Republic of Ezo." However, Ezo was soon after captured by the relentless imperial forces. After a number of battles, Yoshinobu surrendered. The Tokugawa clan was not entirely eliminated, and even their sympathizers would come to hold offices in the new imperial government.

Thus began the Meiji Restoration and the **Meiji period** (1868–1912), officially restoring the unlimited power of governance to the imperial court. Emperor Meiji moved his family to Edo and renamed it "Tokyo" (Eastern Capital). Some former samurai and *daimyōs* were granted offices in the new government, one that its reformers determined would be modern and on par with the powerful nations of the day. They reformed the tax system, lifted the ban on Christianity, and even hired advisers from Western nations to help remake Japan into the powerful nation known today. As a result of the Meiji Restoration, the nation's new manufacturing and industrial economy boomed.

A surge of Japanese nationalism rippled from the Meiji government and Shinto was declared as the official state religion, in which the Emperor was proclaimed to be a living god. In the minds of many Japanese leaders of the day, the only way Japan would truly compete with other major nations would be through expansion and military conquest. It is here that the foundation was laid for Japan's military strategy in the coming world wars.

Of all the reforms of the Meiji Restoration, perhaps the most impactful was the complete abolishment of the samurai class. The wearing of swords was forbidden to all except the national armed forces, whose pay was cut from the stipends given to samurai in the years before the restoration. This dramatic end to Japan's greatest symbol was not taken lightly. How could their swords be taken? Their swords were kept by their pillows at night. They were given swords as children in rite-of-passage ceremonies. It was a symbol of their soul, and the heritage of the country.

Numerous samurai revolts spread like wildfires, leading to the Satsuma Rebellion. Sword-wielding warriors clashed against cannons and firearms. 300 riflemen fell by the sword as General Saigō Takamori led the rebellion of 4,000 samurai and captured the Kumamoto Castle in a last stand of the sword's supremacy. (In fact, stories and video footage exist today of samurai cutting machine guns cleanly in half with their fifteenth-century blades, a testimony to the amazing workmanship and techniques of the medieval swordsmiths.) Yet these last samurai were no match for the imperial troops and the changing face of war.

The Legend of the Last Samurai

Saigō Takamori grew up as a *Gōshi* (lower-class) samurai. His philosophy was simple. He lived to serve his people above himself. As a young man he was an activist for a balanced government, shared between the imperial court and the shogunate before the Boshin War. After the Ansei Purge he was arrested and banished until a *daimyō* pardoned him and sent him to Kyoto to serve on his behalf at the imperial court. With his Satsuma soldiers there, he protected the imperial palace from attacks.

Saigō Takamori could tell that the country was quickly changing and that his desire for a Japan ruled by both the Emperor and the Tokugawa Shogunate would never be a reality. When the last shogun resigned, Takamori knew it wouldn't be enough. He demanded that all of the Tokugawa clan's lands and status must be stripped to prevent a power struggle. Alas, those loyal to the Tokugawa would not consent to such high demands, and the Boshin War began. He fought on behalf of the imperial forces and was the one who captured Edo Castle, effectively ending the destructive conflict.

When Emperor Meiji rose to power, Takamori was given important offices in the new modernized government, including that of ambassador to Korea. With a dedication to the samurai's code of honor, he proposed several measures to his fellow government leaders. He believed these measures were needed to ensure that other nations recognized the Emperor and that Japan's military was given proper budgetary priority. He also had many suggestions on how relations with Europe and North America could be modified to best benefit Japan.

The Meiji government rejected his proposals. Rather than be obliged to make *bushido* their guiding force, they continued to abolish the samurai class and ban the wearing of swords.

Takamori resigned, and later joined the Satsuma Rebellion. His forces originally were armed with modern weapons, but once their ammunition was spent, they battled the imperial forces with the symbols of their heritage, the samurai sword.

It is likely that Takamori knew that the forces he led, and the way of life they represented, were doomed. He may have known that without a dramatic last stand, the ousted samurai class would have endlessly fought for their rightful place. With an intense and terrible end, the new modern government could continue in peace, and the Japanese people would benefit. With his honorable death in the Battle of Sei Nan, he would forever go down in history as the "Last True Samurai."

• • •

As students of swordsmanship, we can learn from the "Legend of the Last Samurai" that even in modern times, one must be true to the spirit of the noble Japanese warrior. Most importantly, we see that a great duelist accepts defeat with honor and dignity.

Although the age of the samurai came to an end in the Meiji period, the spirit of the samurai lives on. Students of kendo faithfully continue their tradition, and their stories will continue to be told in books and in the cinema for generations to come. Most importantly, their code of honor survives in much of Japanese culture. In the next section, we'll take a look at a modern form of this medieval philosophy.

BUSHIDO: THE WAY OF THE WARRIOR

A SAMURAI KNOWN AS JINZAEMON was caught committing a capital offense in the house of his lord, and was sentenced to later be put to death via *seppuku*. While under house arrest, his clan leaders met with him. They asked him about his crimes and if he had any regrets.

Jinzaemon consented that he deserved his coming punishment, but there was one thing that greatly disappointed him. Measures had been taken to prevent his escape. "That it would be thought that a samurai who was in such circumstances would slip underneath a conduit and flee is deplorable," stated Jinzaemon.

A true samurai would never think to escape his rightful punishment. True to the way of the warrior, Jinzaemon met his end honorably, facing his final moments with conviction and dignity.

Yet *bushido* is far more than dying the "right way." It is a code to live by, a philosophy that emphasizes duty above all else, peace in the face of death, the manners of a gentleman, and continual self-improvement. It has been deeply influenced and shaped by Zen Buddhism, Confucianism, Shintoism, and the war-torn history of the samurai. *Bushido* evolved from the many different codes of conduct enforced by various feudal lords in antiquity. Today, it is followed as a tool to navigating the cut-throat business world, as a standard against which to prioritize one's personal responsibilities, and as a guide to living deliberately. It is an insight into Japanese society. Most of all, *bushido* is an invaluable window for the student of swordsmanship into the mind of the samurai.

Note: Great care has been taken by the author in order to faithfully amalgamate the archaic teachings of *bushido* from multiple sources, and present them as generalized precepts that can be implemented in today's society. Consequently, certain era-specific topics and details commonly associated with this code have been left out of this modern interpretation, such as those of suicidal rituals, *daimyō*-related processions, military horsemanship training, and adoptive guardianship. Although in the next sections, the terms "gentleman," "he," and "his" are used, the following principles should not be considered as advice meant only for men.

Duty Above All Else

Virtuous and Selfless Service: An honorable warrior's life is dedicated to the service of others, and he does not consider his life his own. By living his code, the ego is subjugated. He is an example of selflessness to others. In an emergency, he readily shows his loyalty and puts the needs of others before his own. He does not require lavish rewards or recognition. He is reliable, and can be trusted to perform all tasks to his utmost, without excuse. An honorable warrior can always be found engaging in meaningful work. He is worthy of his pay and grateful for it. The honorable warrior is genuine, honest, and true to himself.

Responsibility: If altercations or disturbances arise among his people, an honorable warrior is present to maintain order and keep the peace. To do this, he must first have an orderly and moral mind. Never would he behave like those against whom he defends. His focus is on completing his assignments well, not on what his superiors may think of him. He would never take lightly the matter of requesting time away from his duties. If possible, violence is avoided, as seen in the words of legendary samurai Takeda Shingen: "If you win over a hundred battles, it is not virtue. If you win without battle, it is virtue."

Loyalty to Superiors: Loyalty is one of an honorable warrior's highest virtues. Dedication to his superiors, authority figures, employers, and teachers, is of the highest importance. Even the symbols of his superiors are treated with respect. Proper etiquette is observed in all interactions with those over him. Even when an employer is acting foolishly, the warrior responds with grace and prudence. An honorable warrior never talks back or shows rudeness toward them. Even something that could be indirectly taken as disrespectful is avoided. Important disagreements are handled with the utmost of care. Unimportant disagreements are not discussed.

Devotion to Parents: An honorable warrior is also devoted to his parents, understanding that they are the roots from which he grows and relies. Even in the case of negligent or lackluster parents, he shows his character by honoring and listening to them. It is often the case that a child who does not honor his parents proves useless as a soldier.

Readiness and Diligence: An honorable warrior keeps a mind of readiness. He is prepared, without notice, to perform his duties. If he is called to defend, he already has his sword by his side. When he leaves his home, he considers, with every step, that he is already on the battlefield. He will never assume that all will go as planned. Therefore, he is never surprised. When waiting, he keeps himself occupied with meaningful tasks, and would never be seen with his hands in his pockets, aimlessly sitting, or leaning against the wall. Nor would he ever appear to be resentful of his duties. When not called upon to perform a specific task, a warrior will take upon himself a new discipline and improve his usefulness. Thus he will have so much more the advantage over his peers when called upon in the future.

Professionalism: The honorable warrior does not discuss his personal concerns or familial matters with others while on duty, nor does his mind dwell on them. His interactions with peers is professional and proper. Even in the case where he has a damaged personal relationship with another with which he serves, he continues as if they were still the best of friends.

Grace in Promotion: When an honorable warrior is promoted and made a superior over others, he focuses on the potential, rather than the faults, of those who serve under him. As a leader, he must hold himself to a higher level of self-discipline and accountability. Too often we see the opposite, where his new power is abused, his performance is lackluster, and even more authority is stolen from those higher up in the chain of command. Such behavior is selfish, disgraceful, and dishonest. In times of prosperity or good fortune, the honorable warrior does not forget his duty or his past. He realizes that he is not always the cause for the improvements in his living condition.

Peace in the Face of Death

Keeping Mortality in Mind: The honorable warrior never forgets to consider his own mortality. As a result, even small tasks are performed with serious earnest or *"shin-ken shō-bu."* He doesn't shrink and cower at the thought of his death, but rather uses it to calmly reassess his priorities. The simple beauties of everyday life are appreciated. He is careful not to waste his days, or leave off for the future that which should be done today. He understands exactly how much time is needed to perform what is required of him and plans accordingly. He doesn't gamble with his life by getting into unnecessary fights or thoughtlessly arguing. He is careful and prudent with his safety. He is concerned about his health and does not take his life for granted. He focuses more on living well, rather than only living wealthily. It is his desire to live a full life of service.

Meeting Death Properly: An honorable warrior is not concerned with when he dies. He understands that long life is promised to no one. Rather, he is concerned with meeting death properly, with serenity, dignity, and a dispassionate expression. He doesn't lament being cheated out of some imagined longer life, but accepts that the time has come. Whether on the battlefield, or in a sick bed surrounded by family, his aims are the same. He will take care to ensure his last words are meaningful. Those words should be respected by others.

Bravery: He is filled with bravery, courage, and valor. Cowardice and selfishness have no place in his heart. Should he be called upon to face arrows, gunfire, and certain doom, he will face it boldly and resolutely, meeting his end with honor. Even if he is the last man standing, he will stand his ground, against all odds. In peacetime, an honorable warrior proves his courage by living according to the precepts of *bushido*.

Fierceness in War or Peace: As performing one's duty in peacetime is just as important as the performance of duty in war, the honorable warrior faces his daily tasks and assignments with the same unwavering fierceness he'd show on the battlefield. If a warrior gives a lackluster performance in toilsome or mundane duties in peace, how could he be relied upon in the crisis of war? An honorable warrior performs his duties in peacetime with gratitude. He will not rob himself of satisfaction and reward for a task well done by accepting the new task begrudgingly. Whether it be in small tasks or in great tasks, the same level of dedication and care is given.

The Manners of a Gentleman

Properness: A warrior must live under the highest standards of personal hygiene and cleanliness. His posture is straight, and he has a dignified demeanor. He is well groomed and properly dressed for the season. His clothing is not too costly or extravagant, but is suitable. A personal fan on which to take notes is always kept on his person. He is never without his two swords, even when indoors. Proper seriousness is maintained, even when engaged in ideal hobbies such as hawking.

Politeness: A warrior is sensitive to social customs and exercises proper politeness in all company. Even when eating rice or sipping tea, he does so with dignity and without calling attention to himself. After being invited to a meal by a host, he will not bring with him uninvited guests. When he travels, he will plan ahead accordingly. An honorable warrior is never late, nor does he travel in a hurry.

Abstinence From Slander: Gossip, blame, criticism, and slander are never spoken by a warrior, especially about a peer, superior, or former employer. Not even jokes suggesting such things are told. Even when asked, no slander is given. He understands that he has made mistakes in secret, and would never be so unjust as to point out the deficiencies in others. Even when he is clearly in the right when speaking with a fool, his words are courteous, polite, and dignified. Rather than condemn that which is lacking in another, he chalks it up to inexperience, youth, or poor education. He realizes that speaking poorly of another is also unkind to all who listen.

Thoughtful Speech: An honorable warrior speaks thoughtfully and not too often. His communication is effective, and he avoids discussing matters of which he has little understanding. Likewise, he avoids getting involved in matters that are not rightfully of his concern. He is aware of those who are listening and modifies his conversation accordingly with prudence and respect.

Respect for Others: An honorable warrior shows tremendous respect for his opponents. He does not see them as enemies. Even if he is struck down by them, he bears no grudge against them. He is always in control of his anger. He is never so cowardly as to strike his wife or another who does not have the strength to resist.

Financial Wisdom: Frugality is a major virtue of the honorable warrior. Regardless of his rank, he lives a life of simplicity and shows considerable judgment in all spending. He does not discuss his finances, nor the finances of others, and avoids any dealings with the finances of his superiors. He staves off the poisonous allure of greed. He does not seek to imitate the lifestyles of those with more wealth. Nor does he attempt to have a family of the same size as those of his wealthier peers. Rather, he is content to live within his means and build up his savings. He takes measures to prepare for the unexpected.

Continual Self Improvement

High Personal Standards: An honorable warrior's goal is to always be his best self. Today is the day in which he lives according to his highest discipline and highest level of refinement. In addition, that level is raised, day by day. He strives to be excellent in all he does, and is determined to outperform his peers in at least one field. He strives to accomplish things no one else can do. He is heroic, and performs great deeds that will bring pride to his family and descendants. He will hold himself to high standards, even if his peers do not.

Purity of Heart and Mind: An honorable warrior lives for morality and justice. He holds himself to a high ethical standard, and continually strives to exemplify integrity and moral judgment. Not only does he believe that he should live this way, but he, indeed, lives what he believes, or lives his "inner truth." He does not allow his public or private actions stray one hairsbreadth into unrighteousness. He shows a love of peace and nature. Above all else, he keeps his mind and heart pure with unwavering loyalty, righteousness, and courage. He does not indulge in overdrinking, lasciviousness, laziness, or gluttony.

Perpetual Education: Even in times of peace, the honorable warrior is constantly honing his skills. He is ever the student and ever learning. In addition to his swordsmanship, archery, horsemanship, and martial arts, he studies literature, mathematics, the sciences, the arts, and culture. His mind is sharpened with the study of combat strategy, and he aims to see every problem and setting through the eyes of a strategist. If called upon to lead others, he has properly educated himself beforehand to meet the challenge.

Historical Savvy: History is also an important topic of study to the honorable warrior. He has respect for the nation of his birth and to the country he serves. He honors his family's history and heritage. He also studies the history of those whom he serves.

Progress in Swordsmanship: The pains of grueling practice are well endured by an honorable warrior. He understands that fencing trains in martial skill but also strengthens one's character and diligence. The sword is seen as a tool in the purging of his inner weaknesses. He knows his weapons well. The honorable warrior understands that techniques are to be learned well enough to demonstrate "*Mushin*" (without the mind) so that they can be done reflexively, or automatically, from muscle memory. When one form or style of swordplay is mastered, he will continue on to learn another. After he has proven himself proficient in all of the teachings of one school, he will find another. He will challenge others in non-lethal combat. The honorable warrior is a master to those he defeats, and a pupil to those by whom he is defeated. When he has disciplined himself and has internalized each skill, a thousand opponents on the battlefield may as well be one.

COMBAT SABER LESSONS

THERE IS AN INTERESTING CONNECTION between the history and culture of Japan, and the modern mythology of the Star Wars franchise. Before the creation of Star Wars, writer and director George Lucas was heavily influenced by the foreign films of Akira Kurosawa, such as *Seven Samurai* and *The Hidden Fortress*. Yet that was only the start. The creators of the galaxy far, far away clearly drew upon other Japanese elements for inspiration. This would be most clear in how the characters of the mysterious Jedi were imagined. Their code and philosophy as meditative warrior monks have uncanny similarities to those of Zen Buddhists. In times of war, these servants and peacekeepers would even be called upon to become generals. They are encouraged by their masters to feel, not think, similar to the kendo concept of *mushin*.

The comparisons don't stop there. In the larger Star Wars universe, there are many fictional alien species, such as the Kyuzo, whose culture reflects those of samurai warriors. Planets such as Kamino and Eduu are derivative of Japanese names. And who can miss the helmet of cinema's most iconic villain, Darth Vader, and its close resemblance to the helmet of a Japanese warrior?

For us, the greatest connection between Japan and the Jedi has to do with their fighting style. In preparation for their scenes in which they would duel with laser-swords, the saga's actors were literally trained in kendo. Would you like to be trained in the actual arts of the Jedi? Then you are in luck, because Disney theme parks do offer such official training. However, if you want to dive deeper, below the fictional forms of force-wielding monks, then the place to start is with traditional Japanese fighting styles.

Now that you have an idea of the culture, history, and philosophy behind these techniques, it's time to ignite your saber! All students (regardless of your school or the form being learned) should start off with the "First Five Steps." These steps are the essential lessons that will allow you to learn all others. Once you understand these first elements, learning the lessons that follow will be a piece of cake.

The First Five Steps

Welcome to the new and fast-growing sport of combat saber dueling. Whether you are a young student, eager to prove yourself in fearless combat, the ambitious master of a dojo or club, or simply a parent wishing to train a child up in a new hybrid style of fencing and martial arts, then these lessons will serve you well.

This is the first of five essential lessons all students of the techniques of this sport are encouraged to learn. They are known as the First Five Steps, and go over the basics of combat saber dueling, giving you key information that will prepare you to learn specific attacks, parries, ripostes, and drills in later lessons. What is the best way to grip the saber, stand to face your opponent, step during attacks, or score points? All those questions are answered once you have chosen a specific form to learn, as they all depend on which fencing style you are using.

There are numerous training academies that offer a number of different forms and styles of techniques. Since this manual was created by the Rogue Saber Academy in particular, you will move on to learn the RSA's "Form 1" by lesson 6. From lesson 10 through 66, you'll be trained in individual dueling techniques and practice drills. It is a lot to learn, so feel free to take your time as you progress. Remember your driving force. Have patience with yourself. Remember also that you may capitalize on even the most modest of growth in a match. After all, you'll be able to spar and duel better than most before you even get to lesson 20!

The coming lessons have been designed with extensive research into real-world and well-established techniques. They have each been rigorously tested. Only those shown to be most effective have been included in this manual. It was the intention of the RSA's founders to provide its students with practical techniques that will not only allow them to compete well against all other opponents, but to excel, and to become true champions of the sport.

Of course, that is not to say that techniques taught by other academies are without merit. On the contrary. Every student of swordsmanship can learn something of great value from any other student. Likewise, the greatest saber duelists will be those who study from a broad range of teachers. Once you have mastered all of the RSA's Form 1 techniques, you'll then be encouraged to move on to a new form or school in the true spirit of swordsmanship.

A Note on Left-Handedness: All parts of this manual have been written with right-handedness in mind. Left-handed students will gain a considerable advantage over other students and opponents by mirroring their footwork and adjusting their grip as needed. The targeted zones in each technique, however, should be practiced as they are originally presented.

Common Terminology

Before you can dive too deeply into any school of fencing, it is helpful to have at least a cursory understanding of the meaning behind the following terms:

Lesson: A set of instructions a student of fencing can study on their own, or a presentation that a club leader, dojo master, or parent can share with their student(s) one-on-one, or at a group meeting or class.

Mastery: The level at which a lesson has been fully learned and internalized by a student, as determined by the student and/or by their instructor. Mastery of one lesson is typically required before a student may progress to the next. The use of a lesson's "Mastery Code" may be required to prove one's full comprehension of a particular concept.

Technique: A particular maneuver, usually belonging to its own lesson, that follows established steps instructing you on how to swing your combat saber, move your feet, etc. in order to accomplish a clear objective, such as striking your opponent or defending yourself against a certain strike.

Form: This term is commonly used in three different ways. Traditionally, it refers to a practice routine in which multiple techniques are rehearsed. In the sport of combat saber dueling, however, this term more often refers to an entire family of techniques that are often learned and mastered together. Lastly, this word is also used in reference to the quality of your performance. "Good form" can mean that you are following all instructions well, while maintaining good posture, footwork, control of your saber, etc.

Drill: Like the traditional fencing definition of "form," a practice routine done by a sole duelist, or between training partners, facilitating the rehearsal of multiple specific techniques.

Hit: The moment in which the blade of your combat saber makes (intentional or accidental) contact with your opponent's body.

Strike: The deliberate action in which you successfully hit, or make contact with, your opponent's body, resulting in you scoring a point, if done in accordance with the rules of combat saber dueling.

Slice: A broad sweeping motion of your saber, typically when the hilt is relatively stationary while the tip of the blade travels the greatest distance. It can be loosely compared to the swinging of a baseball bat.

Cut: A motion in which a blade is dragged or slid against a surface (such as an opponent's arm) along the length of the blade. This term may also generally refer to a strike made with the side or shaft of the blade and represents the majority of strikes in this manual.

Stab: Generally, a strike made with the tip or point of a blade in a thrusting, poking, or jabbing motion.

Attack: A complex or simple technique a duelist performs, in which the main objective is to land a successful strike on the opponent and score at least one point.

Parry: A technique employed by a duelist to deflect the opponent's blade, or otherwise prevent them from landing a strike.

Riposte: A technique that begins with a parry, immediately followed by a counter-attack.

Feint: A preparatory action within a technique in which you distract an opponent with your saber's position or with body language. This is done in order to cause the opponent to move their saber or body in a way that exposes them to a surprise attack.

Outside: Typically, a reference to the right side of an opponent, including his/her own right shoulder, right arm, right leg, and so forth. This term originally comes from Western fencing, where duelists face each other side-on, and corresponds to the side of a right-handed opponent away from their front, or "outside" where their body is facing. For our purposes, it is used to emphasize that it is the right side of an opponent from their perspective (not from your perspective).

Inside: Typically, a reference to the left side of an opponent, including his/her own left shoulder, left arm, left leg, and so forth. This term originally comes from Western fencing, where duelists face each other side-on, and corresponds to the front side of a right-handed opponent, or "inside" where their body is facing. For our purposes, it is used to emphasize that it is the left side of an opponent from their perspective (not from your perspective).

Match: An event in which two duelists contend with their combat sabers, using the techniques they have learned against one another.

Spar: A friendly match in which the main objective of both sparring partners is to train and practice.

Duel: An aggressive and competitive match in which each duelist uses the techniques they have learned in an attempt to score more points than their opponent.

Daily Training

These lessons were researched, modified, and written in such a way that an entire dojo of students could be satisfied with mastering just one lesson per day. After a handful of days, you will see a dramatic increase in your ability to win duels. On the other hand, these lessons were also written for simplicity, so that several days are not needed to master a single technique or idea.

However, you should not be too hasty. Students who rush through each lesson, only practicing each technique four or five times, almost always forget old lessons along the way. In order to ensure that your old lessons are not getting lost, practice and master each technique with the recommended number of repetitions. Revisit old lessons often in order to keep them sharp in your mind. In this way, you will not waste time, and your mind will be like a quiver of arrows, filled with techniques, immediately ready for use. Always resist the temptation to skip repetitive practices.

In your path to true mastery, it is recommended that you train with the goal to learn about one lesson per day, over the course of about two and a half months. This allows you time to take a day off to spar and duel with others about once a week.

Of course, this training schedule may be modified by your instructor or master. Likewise if you are a self-taught duelist, you can adjust your own training schedule as needed.

What is a Mastery Code?

Students who record, track, and share their progress perform substantially better than their peers. A "Mastery Code" can help you claim this key advantage!

Each lesson in this manual is paired with a randomly generated code, displayed near the end of the lesson. If you wish to track your personal progress (which is highly recommended), you may do so with your RSA student account. After you have logged into your account, use a simple online form to enter in the code matching the lesson you have mastered. (Be sure to copy it exactly, with proper capitalization.) This will unlock digital rewards and allow you to achieve higher levels and ranks within the community. In addition, a digital training journal on your account will be updated along with an interactive tracking chart that displays the lessons you have completed and those you have yet to complete.

Be sure to ask your instructor or master how he/she would like you to use mastery codes for their particular program.

How to Practice and Master a Technique

In the following lessons, you will find instructions on how to perform a certain maneuver. These instructions focus on three main elements:

- Proper Footwork
- Precise Swordwork
- Correct Breathing

It is your ultimate goal to master each technique so that these three elements are synchronized and inseparable in your mind. Internalize each technique so that you perform all of its steps in one fluid motion, and without having to think about them.

Simply performing a maneuver once or twice will not be enough to properly master it. (Remember, a mastery code should only be used if the technique has become a permanent part of your fighting style, a memory that can be drawn upon with ease in the heat of battle.) In order for such memorization to happen, repetition is key. After you have repeated all of the steps of a technique enough times, the movement will become second nature, and you'll be able to cover all of the steps in one instinctive motion. Only then can you claim the prize of true mastery, utilize the lesson's mastery code, record your progress, and continue in your training. Be sure to pass through these phases in your personal training, for each and every technique you encounter:

1. **Study Phase**: Read through the entire lesson so that each step of it makes sense to you in the context of the overall motion. Alternatively, you may be given these steps by your instructor, in person.

2. **Interpretation Phase**: Carefully perform the technique, slowly checking to be sure your form and execution of each step meets a high standard. Step forward (as the technique requires) and perform the technique against an imagined

opponent, then return back to where you started, only to step forward again to repeat the action. This back-and-forth repeated action is typical of Japanese swordsmanship training. In kendo and kenjutsu it is similar to a type of individual practice (or *Hitori Geiko*) known as *Suburi* and *Joge buri*.

3. **Correction Phase**: Check your form against what is written in the lesson. If possible, review your technique in front of a mirror and/or ask your instructor and fellow students to correct any mistakes you may be making. Be open to their advice, as you certainly do not want to practice a bad habit over and over.

4. **Three-Part Repetition Phase**: Once you feel that you truly understand each movement of the technique, divide it into three easy-to-remember steps (or a beginning, middle, and end). There should be a visible pause between the three steps. Make every repetition count. You would be wasting your time if you simply go through the motions. Every time you perform a technique, make it your best attempt. Perform all three steps ten or more times, until you feel you understand the technique well enough to move on to a new technique. But you are not finished yet!

5. **Two-Part Repetition Phase**: At this point (and only you can tell when you have truly reached this point), you may split all of the parts of the technique into two steps (a "setup" and an "execution"). Perform both steps (stepping forward and back) ten times or more as needed. When you are confident that you could teach this technique to others, then you may move on to the next phase.

6. **Single-Action Phase**: Synchronize all steps, footwork, swordwork, and breathing into one fluid motion. Continue to step forward and back, executing the technique in one

action, repeatedly. Perform this exercise at least ten times, until you feel confident enough to perform this technique within the pressures and challenges of an active duel, and before many spectators. At this point, you should feel that the technique has become a permanent part of you. If that is the case, you may record your progress using the lesson's mastery code, and continue on to the next lesson.

7. **Occasional Review Phase**: From time to time, return to old lessons and spend only a few minutes physically going through each of these training phases. Even at this point, be open to, and grateful for, criticisms and corrections. The ancient teachings behind these techniques can be learned quickly, but there are masters of kendo today, over 90 years old, who practice them daily. Even the greatest masters of the sword see the utility and wisdom in daily practice. Mastering a technique is only the first real step. As is the case with becoming a better person or with building character, mastering the sword is a never-ending quest.

Proper Exercise and Diet

Combat saber dueling is a rigorous sport. If you are not in good health, consult with a medical professional about what steps you may need to take before training in any physical sport.

As a student of this manual, it is expected that you are maintaining a healthy lifestyle. It is recommended that you are drinking plenty of water before, during, and after any training, practice, sparring, dueling, or meditation. As fencing is deeply cerebral, be sure to get plenty of sleep (between six and eight hours) and sufficient daily exercise. If you find yourself too anxious or stressed to learn effectively, engaging in daily relaxation meditation may help.

Whatever your exercise routine, be sure to warm up and stretch beforehand, as well as cool down and stretch afterwards. Exercise every major muscle group, and balance intense cardio with weightlifting according to your needs. Pay attention to your caloric intake, eat plenty of fruits and vegetables, and make sure your diet includes a variety of nutritious foods. It is important to avoid excessive salt, sugar, and fat in your diet.

Spar Often

There is one important and final note that should be considered as you embark upon the epic journey before you. Though it is convenient to learn and practice each technique on your own, it is not sufficient. There are some things that cannot be taught by a teacher. There are some steps that even the most elaborate lessons will miss. Therefore, it is crucial and vital to your education that you invite friends, family members, and/or fellow students of combat saber dueling to spar and practice with you in person.

The RSA provides, on its website, an online platform for finding other students interested in sparring and dueling near you. Even if you are surrounded by fellow students in your club or dojo, take a moment to create an account with the RSA. In that way, less fortunate students can find you, and you will be able to help them in this critical element in their quest to master the combat saber.

Mastery Code: YL9WEV9

Further Study: In this "Further Study" section, found at the end of many lessons in this manual, you will be given terms to look up and study online that correspond with the source material that inspired the particular lesson or technique. You can even bring these terms to your instructor, depending on their area of expertise, for more clarification on one maneuver or another. If you are a master or teacher yourself, this part of a lesson can give you greater insight into how the technique should be taught or performed.

Parts of the Saber

A number of instructions in this manual reference specific sections of the combat saber. Be sure to familiarize yourself with these common terms and descriptions:

Hilt – The metallic handle of the saber is its hilt. It is to be held with gloves and fastened tightly to a blade.

Blade – The translucent polycarbonate segment of the saber, apart from its hilt, is its blade. It is to be illuminated during a duel. It is often detachable, and must be fastened tightly to the hilt.

Blade Tip – At the end of a blade, furthest from the hilt, is its tip. Tips are typically rounded, hemispherical, pointed, conical, or flat. For the purposes of dueling, rounded or hemispherical points tend to be the safest. Blades with damaged tips should not be used in saber dueling.

Last Third – If the blade is divided into three equal parts, the "Last Third" is the section of the blade that is farthest from the hilt, just before the blade's tip. (On a *shinai*, the bamboo sword in kendo, this is referred to as the *Datotsu Bu*.)

Middle Third – If the blade is divided into three equal parts, the "Middle Third" is the section between the first and the last.

Closest Third – If the blade is divided into three equal parts, the "Closest Third" is the section in contact with the hilt and is nearest the wielder's hands.

Balance Point – When you have balanced your entire saber horizontally on the edge of your hand, you've found its balancing point. For most combat sabers and for Japanese swords, this point is on the blade a few fingers above the hilt, at roughly one third of the total length of the saber.

Emitter – The "mouth" of the hilt, or the part of the saber where the hilt meets the base of the blade, is called the emitter.

LED – The light that illuminates the saber's blade is most often one or more LEDs (Light Emitting Diodes). These are typically found within the hilt, usually just below the emitter.

Retention Screw – Near the emitter of most combat saber hilts, one or more retention screws may be found. These fasten the blade within the hilt, and must be tightened properly to avoid injury or damage to property.

Neck – The section of the hilt just below the emitter and retention screws is sometimes referred to as the "neck" of the hilt, and is usually where the right hand grips the hilt.

Activation Switch – Most combat sabers feature a protruding activation switch button on their hilt, that "arms," "ignites," or "activates" the electronics within. Some also double as menu inputs to allow for the selection of various features. In a duel, care should be taken to avoid pressing against these buttons, and a wielder should adjust their grip on their hilts accordingly.

Pommel – The base of the hilt, opposite the emitter, is known as the pommel. Pommels are not to be used against opponents. If detachable, duelists must ensure that their pommels are fastened properly before a duel or spar.

Kill Switch – Like activation switches, kill switches often protrude from the hilts and should be removed prior to a match.

Charging and Data ports – If hilts possess exposed ports for battery charging or for interface with the hilts' software, extra care should be taken to avoid dueling in wet weather, mud or sand.

Belt Clip – Rings, hooks, or protruding nodes may have been added to a saber's hilt (usually near the pommel) to allow it to be worn when it is detached from a blade. During duels or tournaments, duelists are encouraged to remove these (if possible) or take measures to ensure that they do not catch on gloves or clothing.

Respect for the Symbol

In ancient times, a warrior's sword was often considered a symbol of his values, status, lineage, cultural heritage, and important role in society. It was treated with respect, and not as a mere tool of war. As students of combat saber dueling, we tend to be fans of modern myths and pop culture. However, when learning history-inspired techniques, we automatically become students of history (and its caretakers). We step into the shoes of our ancestors, and (if only briefly) glimpse into the lives of the noble swordsmen of the perilous past.

Following in these traditions, all students of combat saber dueling are therefore encouraged to keep their sabers in a place of honor when not in use. They should be cleaned and maintained. If you purchased your saber, it is recommended that you look into advice its manufacturer may have published about how to best care for and maintain your saber. Clean scuffs from the blade regularly. Clean and polish the hilt from time to time. Keep the batteries charged, especially before a partner drill or match. As blades and electronics wear, purchase replacements as needed.

The Signature Flourish

To master this lesson, it is vital that you come to memorize your sword's weight, balance, resistance, flexibility, and overall feel. Just as a baseball player may always keep their mitt within their reach, or a tennis player may sleep beside their racquet, a new student should keep their saber close by. Even the samurai would keep their swords with them while eating, meeting with friends, or shopping.

Give yourself plenty of time and space to whip and swing your combat saber through the air. Slice through imaginary opponents while holding the hilt with one hand and both hands. Get a feel for how fast or hard you can swing it while maintaining safe control. Have a friend hold out their hand, off to their side, as a target while you practice aiming at their palm in stabbing attacks.

Move your saber around your body to prove to yourself that you are able to control it without hitting yourself. Practice stylistic "spins" and "flourishes" to better understand the shifting weight and balance of your saber while it is in motion. While there are countless online tutorials on how to flourish or spin your saber in amusing ways, few of them are actually useful in combat. However, it is good to know some fundamental spins. Be careful and start slow so you don't knock yourself in the back of the head.

Forward Spin:

1. Hold your saber to your right side with one hand. Point its tip upward as your palm faces forward.

2. Grip your saber loosely with all of your fingers except for your thumb, which should create a tight (although incomplete) grip around the hilt. You'll avoid dropping your saber by applying pressure with the base of your index finger as it spins.

3. Tilt your saber back slightly, and whip it forward with enough momentum to allow it to swing in a circle forward, down and back again, to the right of your elbow.

4. Repeat this spin a few times until it becomes natural.

Backward Spin:

1. Hold your saber to your right side and grip it as you would when performing the Forward Spin.

2. Rather than flick the blade of your saber forward and down, you'll keep it pointing mostly to the right, and lean it backward, stirring the pommel of your saber down, away from you, and toward you in a circle.

3. With more practice, you can make the angle of your spin more dramatic so your blade points directly up or down.

A Basic Flourish:

1. Hold your saber in your right hand and point it to the ground, a few inches to the left of your left foot.

2. Perform half of a Backward Spin to point the saber behind you and upward.

3. Trace the tip of your saber diagonally from your upper left to your lower right, spinning it in front of you while crossing your hand to the right. (Shift your weight and move your hips slightly to the left so you don't hit your foot.)

4. Once your saber is pointing down to the right of your right foot, finish the Backward Spin until it points forward.

5. Shift your weight and shift your hips to the right as you complete the flourish, bringing the tip of your saber back to where it started, pointing down and to the left.

6. Repeat these steps and combine them in one fluid motion to perform a basic flourish.

Practice spinning your saber in different directions, adjusting its height and position in reference to your body. This is how you can invent and modify your own stylistic routine. While some schools put a lot of emphasis in teaching a number of different spins, the RSA invites you to focus on creating your own unique "Signature Flourish."

You will perform your signature flourish at the onset of each practice drill and at the beginning of every match in which you compete. It is important that you make it your own, so that any judge or audience member will be able to recognize you from previous events, based upon your identifying spins, flourishes, and movements. Once you have invented and memorized your own unique flourish (lasting just a few seconds), that represents something of your own style and personality, then you may consider this lesson mastered.

Mastery Code: KY6KXMX

Further Study: Notable comparisons can be made between the combat saber and kendo's *shinai*, kenjutsu's *bokutō*, or Iaido's *katana*. For more information on spins and flourishes, feel free to consult the numerous online videos and tutorials on the subject. Some are quite impressive.

Lesson: 3 - The Attentive Stance

It is a mistake to think that swordsmanship is all about movements you make with your hands and arms. Most techniques ahead rely upon the whole body for efficacy, strength, and balance. Although you are not judged based upon your posture in this sport, your form will benefit greatly from remembering it during each attack, parry, and riposte. The mnemonic acronym "STAND" can be useful in remembering how best to have good posture while fencing or listening to instruction:

S – Shoulders should be rolled back, down, and relaxed.

T – Tighten your glutes to support your lower back.

A – Abdominal muscles flex to support your back.

N – Neck straight, especially the back of your neck.

D – Deep breathing, in through your nose and out through your mouth, using your abdominal muscles to do the important work.

The Attentive Stance:

Before any attack or parry with the blade can be learned, all students must acquire the "Attentive Stance" and the "Ready Stance" for their preferred Form. All techniques flow from these starting positions. The Attentive Stance is a student's default, neutral position, and is universally used, no matter what form you are learning. When not practicing, dueling, competing, or dismissed, listen to your instructor while in the Attentive Stance. Remember each of these steps for proper execution:

1. Ensure that your saber is deactivated and pointed downward. (Unless otherwise instructed, all sabers should be "unarmed" in order to not distract from the instructor and to save power.) Hold the hilt so that the blade is

pointing off at a 45° angle to the floor, facing behind you. Keep the tip of the blade close to, but not touching, the floor. The pommel of the hilt would be pointing upward, reaching in front of you to a mid-point between your left side and the center-line of your body.

2. Stand with your feet parallel and shoulder width apart.

3. The left hand holds the emitter of the hilt, almost touching the blade. The blade is pointed backward and downward.

4. Lower the saber to your left side. (Keep the activation switch, if it has one, visible and facing up.)

5. Your left arm is slightly bent naturally as you rest your left hand against your hip bone.

6. Keep your right arm straight at your side. The right hand hangs naturally.

7. Stand up straight. (Think of "STAND.")

8. Eyes are forward and the face is in a neutral expression. Clear your mind and stand ready to listen.

If you are following those steps, then congratulations, you are assuming the Attentive Stance! Memorize and practice the specifications of this stance so that you can get into it in less than two seconds when directed.

Mastery Code: 7FYZS6N

Further Study: This technique is comparable to the "*Shizentai*" and "*Taito*" lessons in kendo.

Lesson: 4 - Sport Rules and Safety

Look at you, you have learned so much! Before completing your "first five steps," it is important to understand how the sport is played, and what important safety measures should be taken in order to ensure that all participants are free from harm.

To master this lesson, locate the most current version of the RSA's official rules for the sport of saber dueling with the RSA's official accompanying "Safety Standards." Be sure to study them both thoroughly, and print off personal copies as needed. They can be found online on the following webpage:

www.roguesaber.com/sport.php

A basic version of these rules and safety standards can be found in the earlier section of this manual entitled, "The Sport of Combat Saber Dueling." If you have already read through them carefully, then you are already a few steps ahead.

The instructor of your particular club or dojo may be operating under a modified version of these rules. Be sure to check with them to ensure that you are training under the same set of rules as the rest of your group.

Mastery Code: U6MPDVL

Lesson: 5 - Proper Breathing, Targeting, and Striking

All techniques in this manual are sorted according to which of the eight "zones" of the body is directly targeted or defended. In fact, in this manual, you will learn at least three different ways to attack and three different ways to defend each target zone. In this lesson, you will be instructed on how to properly aim a strike, avoid "telegraphing" your intentions, the target zones of the sport of saber dueling, proper breathing, and what to do after missing or hitting the intended target.

Before Striking a Target

The proper set up for a successful strike involves breathing in and getting into position. A breath in should be crisp and fulfilling. Breathe in through your nose, sending the air low into your stomach. This movement sometimes naturally occurs when you are raising your arms in preparation for a strike. Taking control of your breathing allows your body to act with greater precision and endurance.

During the downswing, thrust, or dedicated motion that will lead to a successful hit, parry, or riposte, you should exhale. This exhale should be deliberate and supported with the power of your abdominal muscles. Your diaphragm should be engaged. In some fencing disciplines, a strike is accompanied with a hearty shout showing the unification of the duelist's mind, body, and spirit. In this sport, no shout is required, but your breath out should be present nonetheless.

A skilled duelist will never randomly flail in a haphazard attempt to strike an opponent. Rather, he or she will think three or four steps ahead of their actions and rely upon thoroughly practiced reflexes should their plans be interrupted. When you strike, it should be done deliberately and with a clear target in mind.

Of course, the problem with having a clear target in mind is that the angle of your saber's blade, your eyes, facial expression, head movement, shoulder and arm position, stance, and any number of other physical posturing can give away your intentions to an eagle-eyed opponent. When your body language accidentally betrays your plans to your opponent, this is called "telegraphing." Always be mindful of this. Wise duelists limit what they telegraph to a dueling partner. At the same time, they are ever aware of even the most subtle hints given by their partner. Being acutely aware of, and sensitive to, any telegraphing from an opponent takes great skill and practice. Such skill can only come from repeated drills, spars, and duels with multiple opponents.

The Possible Target Zones

Landing a successful strike to any of the following areas will constitute a point, unless a specific location is deemed off-limits for safety reasons such as the head (if no helmet is used), face, eyes, throat, groin, or knees. It would be advantageous to memorize these areas:

HIGH – The head, neck, upper back, and top side of the shoulders, ending at the collar-bone line.

CHEST – The front area between the arms, from the collar bone to the sternum.

CORE – The abdominal muscle area from the sternum to the waist.

LOW – The legs and whole body from the waist down.

OUTSIDE ARM – The right arm from the lower shoulder to the fingertips.

INSIDE ARM – The left arm from the lower shoulder to the fingertips.

OUTSIDE FLANK – The right side of the body from the underarm to the waist.

INSIDE FLANK – The left side of the body from the underarm to the waist.

If You Miss Your Target

Most of the sport of combat saber dueling takes place when an attack is thwarted, or a strike is not successful. That is when your swordsmanship is really tested. If you move to strike a particular target zone of your opponent, and your blade is deflected by a parry, you must be instantly ready for a counter-attack or riposte. In most cases, it is wise to abandon any elaborate plans and move on the defensive immediately. Yet when an opportunity arises, seize it.

Another strategy is to move into each attack with a contingency. Going in with a "Plan B" and "Plan C" can allow you to score a point, even if you miss your first target. If your high attack is parried, you may plan to immediately strike the outside arm. You are not required to retreat back in to the Ready Stance and start over every time you want to make a strike.

If you find yourself missing targets often, that is your sign that you have more practice to do, regardless of how skilled your opponent is. A wise duelist will patiently wait for the best opportunity, then strike true. A missed target shows a lack of mastery or proper planning. Once you have some training and experience, you should no longer allow yourself to simply miss a target. The only reason you should not complete a strike is if you must draw back to defend yourself, or if your attack was successfully parried.

After Striking a Target

Once you have successfully struck the target zone of choice (and earned a point), allow your blade to "bounce" off of your target. Obviously, you should only be employing enough strength to hit your blade against your opponent, not injure them. In a deadly sword match, your motion would be continued through the opponent, or the sword would be drawn back in a path to utilize its cutting edge. In this case, such aggressive force would only add to the chance of injury. Since lingering on the target is not advantageous in a sporting match, it is also important to strike a target and retreat quickly (in most cases). This is done to minimize your exposure to attack.

As you draw back after a strike, re-center your body so that your blade's tip is pointing toward the center of your opponent's head (or as otherwise directed from a particular lesson), even if they are facing an odd angle. Assume the Ready Stance again, or a suitable guard, to protect against a counter-attack.

Breathing should be relaxed and natural after a strike. Quiet and slow breaths help to keep your mind focused, and protect you from surprise attacks meant to interrupt your rhythm.

Mastery Code: A3AM75G

Training in Form 1

In the Rogue Saber Academy, the following techniques are all considered to belong to the same school, method, or set known as "Form 1," "The Two Handed Form," and "The Way of Wisdom." (Your academy, club, or dojo may organize or name these techniques differently.) Elements of this form can be implemented with any weapon, but they are most effective with these types of sabers:

- Common full-length sabers (with straight, cross-guard free, two handed hilts and full-length blades)

- Shortened or "shoto" sabers (with straight, cross-guard free, short "offhand" hilts and shortened blades)

- Heavy dueling sabers (with extra-thick-walled blades or hilts and their resulting added weight)

These techniques complement each other, and are organized according to their practical application (target area, defensive position, etc.) and according to the skill level of the student (Basic, Intermediate, and Advanced.) They were carefully modified to be best implemented in the sport of combat saber dueling, and to be effective against other forms (inspired by other fencing techniques from around the world) and against the techniques of other saber academies, clubs, and dojos.

It should be noted that this form will best serve you when you and your opponent face one another "square-on" or "directly." When dueling an opponent who is standing sideways (pointing one shoulder toward you and one away), roughly 1/3 of these techniques will yield diminished returns. If you find yourself dueling such opponents, keep in mind that these maneuvers will land on slightly different target zones but will work well for you nonetheless.

Each of the techniques of Form 1 is based upon East Asian and Japanese fencing styles. The strongest influence has come from the modern martial art of kendo, the broad school of kenjutsu, and the refined *katas* of iaido. More information about each of these particular schools of swordsmanship can be found in the "Ways to Continue Your Training" chapter near the end of this manual.

Speaking in broad terms, Japanese sword techniques tend to be inseparable from the serious warrior spirit inherited from the honor-bound samurai of antiquity. They differ from Western fencing styles in many notable ways. For example, solid footing is emphasized in order to provide a foundation for powerful downward blows. Duelists typically face their opponents square on, with a two-handed grip on their swords. Proper attitude and respect for the sword are always present in the mind of a Japanese swordsman. Japan's modern culture, identity, and heritage, in many ways, are interwoven with its unique fencing traditions.

Although the techniques in this form are heavily modified to be used in an unrelated sport, and with a weapon resembling a science fiction device, the historical core of each technique should be handled honorably and with proper respect to their origins. In order to fully master this lesson, take a moment to research the samurai, *bushido*, and the history and culture of Japan. (If you have already studied the sections of this manual on Japanese history and the code of the samurai, you are already ready to move on!)

Mastery Code: GD4RPZS

Lesson: 7 - Form 1 Two Handed V-Grip

In this lesson, you'll learn how to properly hold your saber's hilt to allow for the best versatility and results. The terms "V-grip" and "chambering" are also explained.

The V-Grip: While holding your combat saber's hilt, both hands are like mirror images of each other, working as a team. As one hand pushes, the other pulls. Follow these steps to ensure that your combat saber is held suitably in order to maximize your ability to perform all of the included techniques. If you are not right-handed, feel free to switch the hands in each step as needed:

1. Twist your saber, if necessary, so that its activation switch is pointing directly away from your chest. (If you accidentally switch off your saber and strike an opponent, no point is awarded. In such an instance, be sure to reignite it right away.)

2. Set the hilt into the heel (or thickest part of the palm) of your left hand. (Your left arm and the hilt should make a 45° angle.)

3. Wrap your left hand's fingers around the pommel and lower portions of the hilt. Your left hand controls the major, broad movements of the saber, therefore your grip with your small finger, ring finger, and thumb are tight around the base of the hilt. Your index and middle fingers are semi-relaxed.

4. From your side, approach the hilt with your right hand at a 45° angle. Grasp the neck of your combat saber, a finger's width (or so) below its emitter.

5. Your right hand will control the minor, precision movements of the saber. Therefore, the grip with your right hand doesn't need to be as strong as the grip with your left.

Tighten your grip with your middle finger, ring finger, and thumb, while allowing your index finger and small finger to be semi-relaxed.

6. Ensure that your thumbs and index fingers create acute V shapes. (A baseball-bat style grip at a 180° angle is not practical for this form.) As you practice, you will find that this is the most practical, natural, and comfortable way to hold the saber.

Chambering: In a few of this form's techniques, you will be directed to "chamber" your saber. This is often done in preparation for a vertical or horizontal slice. To chamber your saber, point its tip straight up. Back the hilt so that its emitter is less than an inch away from your shoulder. The palm of your right (upper) hand should be facing into your shoulder. Both forearms should remain horizontal and parallel to each other. Chambering can be done against each shoulder, hip, or even overhead. When done on a hip or overhead, the blade tip should be pointed backward. If you chamber back on the right shoulder or hip, the right foot should be stepped back, and vice versa. It is a preparatory movement, optimizing your ability to make a clean strike. Practice chambering your saber into either shoulder a few times. This will allow you to transition into it more smoothly in the future.

Master this lesson by picking up your saber's hilt (with its blade attached) several times. Transition into the V-Grip in as few steps as possible, until you are in the habit of automatically holding the hilt with both hands properly.

Mastery Code: 5GNQPWX

Further Study: This technique is comparable to the common instructions you will find on the proper gripping of the *shinai* in kendo or the *katana* in kenjutsu. Chambering can be seen in the "*Hassou* Stance" in kenjutsu.

Lesson: 8 - Form 1 Ready Stance and Footwork

The Ready Stance

This stance is great for offering offense as well as defense. You will assume this starting ready stance, a "middle guard position," immediately before any practice, duel, or competition when using these techniques. Be sure to practice it until you are comfortable transitioning into it as a reflex rather than as a memorized sequence of movements. You will transition from the Attentive Stance by swinging the saber forward, holding the hilt with both hands, and by stepping forward in one fluid motion. You will find yourself returning to this position frequently in a duel prior to, and after, the execution of various techniques.

1. Assume the Attentive Stance.

2. Breathe in. With your eyes still facing forward, activate your saber's switch with your left thumb. (Alternatively: If you cannot reach the switch with your left thumb, you will memorize the position of the switch so that it can be activated with your right hand in the next step without having to look at the hilt.)

3. Bring your right hand (thumb pointing back) over to your hilt and slide it under most of your left hand, clasping the hilt.

4. Release the hilt with your left hand.

5. Twist your right wrist (the knuckle of your small finger pointing downward) so that the blade points behind you, up and forward, its tip finally pointing between the eyes of your

(actual or imagined) opponent. The saber hilt and blade should be vertically centered with your body. Breathe out.

6. Grip the pommel or bottom of the hilt with your left hand so that the bottom edge of the saber fits inside your left palm. Ensure that your left hand is one or two fist-sizes in front of your body.

7. Step your right foot forward. Your right heel should be as far forward as your left toes. You should have the space of the width of one of your feet between your feet.

8. Slightly lift the heel of your back foot and bend your right knee.

Your shoulders are to remain relaxed, and your arms and elbows should be against your body. Keep your wrists in line with your hands and arms. Your grip on your saber must be tight, but not so tight that you restrict blood flow to your hands. Your body weight should be equally balanced between your front and back foot.

Be sure to always keep your eyes trained on your opponent or instructor. Your foot should be moved forward, in a fluid motion, at the same moment that the tip of your blade points to your opponent's eyes. Avoid the bad habit of sliding your feet backward or forward after your blade is already in place. The transition from the Attentive Stance to the Ready Stance should be precise and quick. If you find yourself taking longer than two seconds, continue to practice. Your blade should not be leaning to one side or the other, and your arms should be pressed inward, against your body.

Check your V-grip and your posture. (Remember: STAND.) Finally, when the tip of the blade has been "whipped" into position, make sure that the saber is held tight so that the tip of the blade does not wander. Rather, it should instantly be frozen into position. You may practice these gripping techniques by letting go of your saber with one hand, and then returning it. If your hand lands incorrectly, adjust it as needed. Alternate which hand you remove until you are grasping the hilt properly on the first attempt.

The Home Position and Footwork

Keep your right foot a natural step ahead of your left so that the back of your right heel is in line with the front of your left toes. There should be the width of your foot between both feet. Raise your left heel slightly off of the ground. This is the default position for your feet, or the "Home Position." Instructions on how to step and move vary from lesson to lesson. However, in this form, there are two main types of footwork to learn: "Walking Step" and "Primed Step."

Walking Step: This is the natural pattern you would follow when casually walking. Step with your forward foot, then shift your weight onto it as you pick up and step forward with your other foot. The heel of your forward foot should land a few inches in front of the toes of your back foot.

Primed Step: When you step forward, push off from your back foot and slide your right foot forward. The right foot should glide, barely off of the ground, before touching down. Your left foot should then slide forward immediately after to maintain the home position as often as possible. This return of the second foot should be a quick "snapping" movement. When stepping back, slide the left foot back, and then allow the right foot to "catch up" so that you, again, ensure that your feet return to the default home position.

This footwork is the standard, but is not the rule. In many of the lessons to come, you will be instructed to perform footwork that goes against this basic pattern. However, unless otherwise directed, you should still attempt to maintain this home position as persistently as possible.

Why slide the feet? Hovering the feet just above the ground allows for speed, but also a footing stable enough to avoid being knocked over or easily overwhelmed. Therefore, you will not see many skipping or jumping movements in this form. This is doubly true in this swordsmanship style—precision is key and excessive movement is to be avoided.

Primed Step can be practiced by taking two steps forward and then two steps back. With each movement, the second foot returns to its position relative to the other. Do this until you can step with this pattern instinctively.

Mastery Code: LDZBZCF

Further Study: The Ready Stance is comparable to the *"Chudan Kamae"* in kendo and the *"Seigan* Stance" in kenjustu. Walking Step footwork is comparable to *"Ayumi-ashi"* in kendo. The Primed Step footwork and the Home Position are comparable to kendo's *"Suri-ashi"* and *"Okuri-ashi."*

Lesson: 9 - Form 1 Meditations

Students of this form are encouraged to engage in private mindfulness meditations for about 15 minutes each day. Doing so calls back to the group meditation sessions often facilitated by kendo instructors before lessons or practices. It also allows the student to consider the philosophies at the roots of the culture of the samurai.

In order to master this lesson, refer to the "Meditation Lessons" section of this manual. There you will find basic, intermediate, and advanced techniques that correspond with the three types of dueling lessons that follow. Try out each technique at least a couple of times. If one works well for you, you are encouraged to continue utilizing it throughout the duration of your study of this form.

Mastery Code: Z66MH3V

Basic Techniques

In order to master this lesson, simply make sure that you understand its contents so that you have a good idea of what to expect in the lessons to come.

The first third of the techniques you'll learn are classified as "Basic." It is strongly recommended that all students start with mastering these lessons before moving on to the intermediate and advanced techniques. By the time you've reached this lesson, you are not expected to have yet been in any spars, duels, or tournaments. However, you should have built or purchased at least one combat-ready saber and have mastered the First Five Steps.

Students of the RSA would have typically reached the rank of "Initiate" in the Rogue Order before completing this lesson. If you belong to a club or dojo, check with your instructor to see if you are deemed ready to move on in their program before studying the basic techniques.

Basic Attacks:

The first lessons you will come across are all "Direct Attacks." This is the simplest form of attack. In other words, they are techniques you use proactively, without necessarily any particular prompt. In fact, it is best if you move in on your own timing when you see a clear opportunity to score a point. You will select a target, move directly to that target, score a single point, then retreat. You'll learn more elaborate attacks later, but these solid techniques will serve you well, even in your fiercest duels.

Basic attacks are based upon the "preemption from a state of suspension." Before making your strike, your mind and body are serene, calm, and in control. When the moment to attack arises, you are swift and powerful. Strike quickly and with full purpose. Aim to hit the target, and do not allow yourself to miss. These maneuvers are most effective against opponents who are still making up their minds on what to do. When practicing direct attacks, make sure to practice well, with seriousness and a dedication to perfect form. These techniques are useful in starting duels and making time your ally.

Basic Parries:

Following the basic attacks, you'll learn eight parries to protect yourself from an attack to each of your eight target zones. A parry is also known as a "guard" or "block." If you were to ask a teacher of kendo, Kenjutsu, or iaido about parries, they may not have much advice to give, since parries are traditionally seen as transitions between techniques, not techniques themselves. Ideally, once you stop an attack against you, you should automatically launch a counter-attack (or "riposte") against your opponent. Yet in this introductory level, you'll first learn how to stop your opponent from scoring a point against you. This is in the Japanese tradition of "Killing the sword," or *Ken wo korsu*,"in which a duelist focuses on gaining the upper hand by knocking their opponent's sword off center. After mastering all basic techniques, you'll graduate on to learn effective ripostes.

Mastery Code: NFYRR6W

Further Study: On techniques like these, feel free to look up "Striking Down an Opponent in a Single Beat" and "The Single Stroke" in the *Water Scroll*, as well as the "Three Preemptions" in the *Fire Scroll*, of Musashi's *Book of Five Rings*. Looking into *"Sen-no-sen," "Tobikomi Waza," "Shikake Waza,"* and *"Debana Waza"* in kendo can also be helpful.

Form 1 Basic High Attack

Summary: When fully mastered, this technique is the "crown jewel" of kendo, and can be used with devastating effectiveness. It is the most fundamental of kendo strikes, and modifications of it produce all other attacks. Even the most skilled duelists return to it in a pinch, due to its simplicity and usefulness. It is important to note that in combat saber dueling, this particular strike must be modified according to whether or not both combatants are wearing helmets. If they are, the top of the helmet is targeted. Otherwise, this technique targets and strikes the outside (right) shoulder of an opponent (picture a monarch "knighting" a brave soldier). While stepping forward, raise your saber above your head and swing downward in a vertical slice, targeting the closest shoulder of your opponent with the last third of your blade before stepping back into the ready stance.

Execution:

1. Assume the Ready Stance.

2. Slide your right foot forward (slightly to the left of your opponent's blade), pushing off from your back foot which remains firmly planted. Your right knee should be slightly bent.

3. Breathe in. Lift your saber straight up, using mostly your left hand, elbows pointing naturally away from the face. The tip of the blade should be centered, pointing straight up, and not to the side. Keep lifting the saber up until the blade tip is pointing straight behind you, and your hilt is directly over your head.

4. As you slide your left foot forward (so that your feet are back in the home position), slice your saber downward in a

straight and controlled vertical line so that the tip of your saber strikes your opponent's outside shoulder (or helmet). Breathe out. (The tip should flick into place like the cracking of a whip. However, it is important that you do not execute this motion with too much force, or else you may injure your opponent.)

5. Slide your left foot backward and follow it with your right foot so that it remains one step ahead of your left. Keep your guard up, and return to the Ready Stance.

Checking Your Form: Keep your shoulders relaxed. While your blade is coming down, make sure that your arms remain tight against your body and that you squeeze the hilt tightly to slow and stop its motion. The strength and "flick" of this movement comes from your wrists, which should remain in line with your arms. Do not let your wrists bend too much so that you lose that strength. When the strike is made, your right thumb should be pointing toward your opponent. In your practices, watch the tip of your blade as you swing your saber to make sure it is slicing in a clear straight line. Do not let it swerve or point in an odd direction. Throughout every step, maintain good posture.

Mastery Code: K97DAJ5

Further Study: This technique is comparable to the "*Men-uchi*" or "*Migi-Men* Strike" in kendo and the "*Daijyoudan* grip," "*Makkou* slice," and "*Shomen Uchi*" in kenjutsu.

Lesson: 12 - Plasma Stab

Form 1 Basic Chest Attack

Summary: Although all students should learn this stabbing attack, it should only be used against others (in practices or in competition) when suitable armor is worn to protect against it. This is a basic technique but can potentially be one of the most dangerous. Therefore, only a student with complete confidence in their mastery of it should use it in a spar or duel. Pointing a saber directly at an opponent's chest is an aggressive and intimidating gesture. Since it can be carried out quickly, this maneuver is a favorite among the most ruthless and sly of students. If your opponent shrinks back or retreats as a result of this attack, you have gained the upper hand.

Execution:

1. Assume the Ready Stance. Ensure that your saber's hilt is drawn in, near your stomach.

2. For safety reasons, make sure that your opponent is NOT moving toward you, but is standing still or retreating.

3. Breathe in. Push off from your left foot for a medium-sized step, sliding your right foot forward.

4. Bring your arms forward (not just your hands). Rather than raise or lower your saber, it should be shooting forward like a controlled rocket. The main thrust must come from your left hand.

5. As your right foot touches the ground, and with the tip of the blade, make brief contact with your opponent's chest and pull back immediately. Breathe out.

6. Pull your right foot back. Return to the Ready Stance.

Checking Your Form: Stabbing techniques are best done as interruptions between your actions and your opponent's actions. While thrusting forward, keep your thumbs pointing forward and in line with your wrists. Your wrists should also stay in line with your arms. Your saber should not travel any further forward after your right foot meets the ground. Rather, your forward step and "stab" should happen at the same time. When practicing, be sure to thrust your saber straight forward, and not off at an odd angle. If dueling or sparring against armored female opponents, aim high on the chest, near the shoulders.

Mastery Code: TR622VR

Further Study: This technique is comparable to the "*Morotetsuki*" strike in kendo. See also the "Stabbing the Face" and "Stabbing the Heart" techniques in the *Water Scroll* of Musashi's *Book of Five Rings*.

Form 1 Basic Core Attack

Summary: This is the tamer "younger brother" of the previous technique, and targets the core. Nevertheless, the same safety precautions apply. Although all students should learn this stabbing attack, it should only be used against others (in practices or in competition) when suitable armor is worn to protect against it. It is easy to execute, but also equally easy to defend against, so it is best utilized when your opponent is fatigued or not paying attention. Slide your blade along your opponent's, as if falling into a monster-infested pit, until it reaches their hands, and thrust into their abdomen.

Execution:

1. Assume the Ready Stance.

2. Use the middle third of your blade to briefly apply subtle pressure to the left side of your opponent's blade, from your perspective. (Close the distance between you with small steps beforehand, if necessary.)

3. Before your opponent can respond, slide your saber down along their blade. (Be aware of their blade's position. Since you are applying pressure to its side, it should remain safely off to your right or down as you perform this technique.)

4. Breathe in. Slide your right foot forward (slightly to the left of your opponent's blade from your perspective), pushing off from your back foot which remains firmly planted.

5. Extend your arms forward (as if pulling an imaginary string out of your stomach) and tap the tip of the blade against their stomach. Breathe out and immediately pull back.

6. Step both feet back and return to the Ready Stance.

Checking Your Form: Prolonged contact with an opponent's blade is always risky. Be mindful that your blade may be knocked down or to the side. To minimize the risk of deflection, this technique is best performed quickly. When practicing, imagine that your opponent's saber is held in the Ready Stance and is pointing toward your eyes.

Mastery Code: 4QR5WRX

Further Study: This technique is comparable to the general *"Tsuki"* stab in kenjutsu and the *"Suriage Waza"* in kendo.

Form 1 Basic Low Attack

Summary: Far from the noble ways of kendo, this technique is derived from obscure kenjutsu methods. Generally, targeting the legs is avoided in fencing because doing so may leave the head unprotected. You may be good in a fight, but you won't be able to talk your way out of this one! Instead, you'll find a way to steer clear of any imminent riposte. Charge past the side of your opponent (smuggling your saber), and swing your blade back to strike the back of one leg.

Execution:

1. Assume the Ready Stance.

2. Breathe in. Starting on the right foot, sprint using regular Walking Step to the left side of your opponent (from your perspective), until your right shoulders are side-by-side. (Speed is key, and you should not have to take more than three steps.) Keep your combat saber up and to your right side to defend against attack.

3. Once you have stepped behind your opponent, release your left hand's grip on your saber. Step diagonally to your right with your right foot. Turn your face to the right and follow your saber with your eyes.

4. With only your right hand, swing the saber diagonally downward, past your right side, striking the muscular back of the lower right leg (the calf muscle) of your opponent. Breathe out.

5. Suspend your saber in place, and center your body around it (pivoting on your right foot). Return to the Ready Stance.

Checking Your Form: When you are swinging the saber downward, it will feel more like throwing it than striking with it. Aim low, and be extra careful so as not to strike the front, side, or back of the knee.

Mastery Code: ME44LG6

Further Study: This technique is comparable to one-handed "*Hidari Kesa Giri*" and back-handed slices in kenjutsu.

Form 1 Basic Outside Arm Attack

Summary: If done with the mythical laser-sword, this technique would sever your opponent's right hand at the wrist, leading to an all but certain victory. Yet for our purposes, you'll simply be able to score a point by swinging your blade up and landing its last third on your opponent's forearm, just above the wrist. It is similar to the Knight's Strike, yet different in that the needed reach of your saber and distance traveled is not as great. Therefore, it can be done with greater speed.

Execution:

1. Assume the Ready Stance.

2. Breathe in. Take a shorter-than-usual step forward (and slightly to your left) with your right foot.

3. Lift your saber straight up, elbows pointing just a few degrees off from directly forward. Only lift the saber far enough so that the middle of the hilt is just above your eyes. Twist on your right foot so that your body is facing your opponent's outside forearm.

4. As you catch your left foot up, slice your saber downward in a straight and controlled vertical line so that the last third of the blade hits directly on the lower forearm of your opponent, just above their wrist. Breathe out.

5. Draw your body and the saber straight back (rather than lift the saber upward) in a slicing motion. Step the left foot back.

6. Follow back with your right foot into the Ready Stance.

Checking Your Form: The moment your blade meets the arm of your opponent, squeeze your hilt tightly in order to make the strike with better precision.

Mastery Code: 4X6H5YE

Further Study: This technique is comparable to the *"Kote-uchi"* in kendo.

Form 1 Basic Inside Arm Attack

Summary: With this technique, you will target your opponent's left arm, just below the shoulder, with a diagonal slice that would be used to cut someone in two from their left shoulder to their right flank with a sword. You will bring your right side back with your saber, then swing your right side forward, slicing diagonally downward. This maneuver is especially handy against clones attempting to betray you.

Execution:

1. Assume the Ready Stance.

2. Breathe in. Step your right foot backward while chambering your saber back into your right shoulder. (Keep the saber vertical, with the neck of the hilt almost touching your shoulder.)

3. Pivot on your left foot and swing your right side forward as you take a giant step toward the right of your opponent (from your perspective).

4. While stepping forward, push your saber up and forward with both arms. Swing the last third of the blade from above and the right, so that it hits your opponent's left arm (just below the shoulder). Breathe out.

5. Follow through with the slice, while gliding your right foot back into the home position. Bring the hilt of your saber down to your stomach in the Ready Stance.

Checking Your Form: When you step back, do not twist or turn your body. Rather, keep facing directly forward. Be sure not to raise your right shoulder as you chamber your saber. Chambering your saber should build tension, like loading a spring. When making the attack, your saber should "spring" up and forward from your shoulder, releasing all tension.

Mastery Code: YGWMHF4

Further Study: This technique is comparable to the "*Hassou Stance*" and "*Migi Kesa Giri*" in kenjutsu.

Form 1 Basic Outside Flank Attack

Summary: Like a business negotiation with a vile gangster, a good strike comes with patience and the aggressive seizure of an opportunity. Chamber your saber back into your left shoulder. Once an opening is found, horizontally swing your saber squarely against the right flank of your opponent.

Execution:

1. Assume the Ready Stance.

2. Breathe in. Pull your saber into your left shoulder so that it is chambered. The emitter should be at about mouth level and the blade should point straight upward.

3. Pivot on your right foot and take a large left step forward (pulling your right side back and away from any danger) and swing your saber horizontally into your opponent's outside flank.

4. Strike the flank of your opponent at a perpendicular angle.

5. Pull your saber backward while slightly twisting it clockwise. Step your left foot back and return to the Ready Stance.

Checking Your Form: Keep your eyes forward and focused on your opponent at all times. When chambering your hilt into your left shoulder, keep your left shoulder low and relaxed. When stepping forward into the horizontal swing, do not hunch or duck your head. Keep your posture upright as you fully extend the right arm. Point your left elbow downward while making the horizontal slice.

Mastery Code: G9J3THY

Further Study: This technique is comparable to the "Reverse *Hassou* Stance" and "*Hidari Ichimonji Giri*" in kenjutsu.

Form 1 Basic Inside Flank Attack

Summary: If your style has become predictable, this is a good way to keep your opponent guessing. This technique targets and strikes the inside (left) flank, using a backward C-shaped downward swing, while taking a retreating step back. Slice down as if you were using a pickaxe. But rather than finding a crystal, you'll be awarded with a point!

Execution:

1. Assume the Ready Stance.

2. Take small primed steps forward while maintaining the home position. (This is done to eliminate some of the distance to your opponent and apply some psychological tension.)

3. Breathe in. Shift your weight to your right foot and raise your saber vertically so that your hilt is just above your eyes.

4. While taking a step backward with your left foot, swing your blade down and to the right, finally hooking back into the left flank of your opponent. Breathe out.

5. Pull your saber straight back, along with your right foot, and return to the Ready Stance.

Checking Your Form: It is common for students to want to roll the shoulders forward or hunch when attacking while stepping back. It is important to keep good posture in mind. Your saber should hit its target at the same moment your left foot touches down. While practicing, imagine your opponent to be just barely in reach of the tip of your saber. In that way, you will not be surprised with the difficulty of reaching your opponent when performing this technique in a spar or duel.

Mastery Code: 56X8S2Y

Further Study: This technique is comparable to *"Hiki-waza"* and the *"Gyaku-dou-uchi"* in kendo.

Form 1 Basic Attack Pattern Drill

Summary: In this drill, you will combine every technique you have learned so far. In this case, you will not require a partner. However, students have found it easier to learn drills such as this, when a friend reads through the movements as they are performed. Each technique will be executed in smooth succession, as if you are cutting down a group of invisible enemies. Feel free to imagine any variation of saber-wielding assassins, jinxed objects, robots, imperial troops, or monstrous creatures surrounding you as you complete each movement. (For clarity, "Clock Position" orientation is used in the description of these drills. Simply imagine yourself standing on a large analog clock to make sense of the directions.) Give yourself plenty of room. Practicing this drill outdoors is preferable. Start out by performing each technique and transition slowly, and then work up to doing it at full dueling speed. Once you can complete this entire drill from memory without pausing or making a mistake, you will have proven to yourself that you are ready to continue on with your training.

Execution:

1. Begin in the Attentive Stance, facing front (at 12:00), and standing in the "center point" of your practice space. Bow to the approaching horde of six enemies, activate your saber, and salute to them with your signature flourish.

2. Transition into the Ready Stance. Picture two enemies, rushing to face you.

3. Slide both feet forward in Primed Step, performing the **Knight's Strike** on the right shoulder of your first enemy, slicing it down to its waist. As he falls to your left side, prepare for the second, just behind. Rather than sliding both feet back to the starting position, immediately advance.

4. Take a medium-sized right step further forward (at 12:00) to execute the **Plasma Stab**, piercing it through the chest. Pull your saber back sharply to free your blade. A third enemy is now attempting to surprise you from the right, aiming to stab you in the face. When you retreat your right foot back, pivot on your left to turn your body 90° to your right, so that you are now in the Ready Stance facing 3:00. Your turn caused your saber to meet and redirect the third enemy's blade, placing you both toe-to-toe.

5. As you stand close to your enemy, demonstrate the **Pitfall** by sliding down their blade and impaling their stomach. Unstick your saber as you retreat with one step back into the home position.

6. The third enemy, clutching its stomach, still lumbers forward, swinging wildly. Dash with two steps diagonally to their right (with the Walking Step, toward 2:00) and swing back, chopping their right leg with the **Smuggler**. Keep your saber pointing low to the ground and re-center yourself (to face the center point). As you turn, you see two foes side-by-side, who were just behind you.

7. First, target the fourth foe, the enemy on the left side (from your perspective). Avoid a vertical slice from the fifth by taking a large step with your right foot to the left side of the two. Assume the Ready Stance, then disarm the fourth foe with the **Hand Slice**.

8. Just as your saber cuts off the fourth enemy's right hand, the fifth foe attempts to slice through both of your hands. Quickly pull back your arms and saber. Continue to take a large step back with your right foot, turning your body. Chamber your saber up into your right shoulder, and while the fifth foe's saber swings to the ground, slice them in half with the **Clone Cutter**. In a wide stance, bend your knees as

you follow through with the slice. Bring the hilt of the saber to your left hip as the blade tip points downward.

9. The last of the horde, the sixth, quickly comes to the side of the fourth, who is fumbling on the ground in order to pick up their fallen saber. Chamber your saber into your left shoulder in preparation.

10. Before the sixth comes any closer, you charge toward them with a step from your left foot, and then from your right (facing 9:00), and utilize the **Hut Slap** to horizontally slice them in half.

11. Turn to face the center point.

12. Now armed with their saber in their remaining hand, the fourth enemy's saber clashes against yours. Great pressure is applied against the sabers. They attempt to push you back and down, but you push them back, walking toward 6:00 until you return to the center point.

13. Finally, you pull back and perform the **Crystal Mine**, dividing their torso from their lower body, thus defeating the last of the enemies.

14. Straighten your posture, turn to face 12:00, and return to the Ready Stance.

15. Deactivate and spin the saber down and back to your left hip as you transition into the Attentive Stance.

16. Complete the drill with a bow.

Mastery Code: GXGFJ4K

Further Study: This drill is comparable to *"Hitori Geiko"* and entry-level *kata* sequences in kendo, Kenjutsu, and iaido.

Form 1 Basic High Parry

Summary: The most simple of defensive movements is the evasive step. Since it is so simple, a preemptive riposte (with movements similar to those of the Hand Slice) has been added as a bonus feature to this lesson. Your main goal is to side-step in order to bring your body out of the alignment with an opponent's attack to your "high" target zone. Although a frequently used technique, it should be understood that it should only be done to place you in a privileged position to strike. If you retreat and still find yourself in a compromised position, then you are all but guaranteed your opponent's victory. Therefore, in this lesson, you will be walked through a proper evasion and counter-attack.

Execution:

As your opponent attempts to strike down to your head, neck, or shoulders from above...

1. Push off from your left foot in order to take a diagonal step forward, and to your right. (This step should be just large enough to place you out of harm's way, but no larger.)

2. As you step, breathe in and raise your saber up so that its emitter is in front of your face. (This is to avoid any contact with your opponent's blade.)

3. As your left foot catches up, pivot on your right foot to face your target square on. Slice your saber downward in a straight and controlled vertical line so that the tip of your saber strikes your opponent's inside (left) shoulder, or their shoulder closest to you. (Alternatively, if they are wearing a helmet, strike the top of the head.) Breathe out.

4. Return to the Ready Stance.

Checking Your Form: Maintain good posture. As is the case with many parries, ripostes, and counter-attacks, your efficiency of movement and use of time is important. If you take too large a step, you will signal to your opponent to go on the defensive. If you swing your blade too high, you could lose valuable time. Your downward strike should make contact at the exact same time that you would have been hit if you did not step aside. Keep your movements in this technique as small and concise as possible to take advantage of the recovery time needed by your opponent to react. If practicing without a partner, use a chair or other stationary object to represent an opponent.

Mastery Code: XBUQV32

Further Study: This technique is generally comparable to "*Nuki Waza*," or the "*Men-Nuki-Men Kata*" in kendo.

Form 1 Basic Chest Parry

Summary: Whenever an opponent advances toward you, they step into a higher level of danger by closing the distance between you both. In this technique, you will take advantage of that and intercept them by standing your ground, "deflecting" their blade, and scoring a point. The following directions are for the case in which your blade is on the right side of your opponent's blade (from your perspective.) In a situation where this is not the case, simply use your left foot to step forward and mirror all other movements as necessary. As done with the previous parry, a bonus counter-attack is included in this technique.

Execution:

As your opponent attempts to strike you with a stabbing motion to your chest...

1. Keep your feet planted, and (with no more pressure than needed) press against the side of their incoming blade so that its tip passes safely off to your left side.

2. Breathe in. While maintaining pressure on their blade, take a small step forward with your right foot. (This step is not to thrust or get you closer to your opponent. Rather, it is to enable you to sink your body lower. Bend your knees as needed.)

3. Twist your body so that your right shoulder is facing into your opponent. Your right foot should be pointing toward them, while your back foot should remain perpendicular.

4. Slide your blade down your opponent's so that both saber hilts are only a foot or so apart.

5. While keeping their saber blade safely pointing away from you, angle the tip of your saber down (making a scissor-cutting motion with your blades) so that it makes contact with your opponent's chest. Breathe out.

6. Take a large step back with your left foot, and only relieve the pressure from your opponent's blade after you have returned to the Ready Stance.

Checking Your Form: This parry is most effective when done with minimal movement. In fact, if done correctly, your opponent will step into your blade's tip as part of their thrusting motion, requiring only a minor step toward them on your part. Keep your arms tight against your body, using the strength in your chest and core to absorb any returning pressure from their blade. Avoid taking too large a step at the beginning so as not to jeopardize your ability to step back after the point is earned. This particular technique is difficult to practice without a partner, so be sure to follow each step as exactly as possible.

Mastery Code: RBM5CYZ

Further Study: This technique is comprised of a number of counter-stabbing methods in kenjustu, and utilizes kendo's "*Suriage Waza.*"

Form 1 Basic Core Parry

Summary: A personal favorite of the author, this iconic parry turns an opponent's manipulation of your blade immediately against them. When their blade is pressing against yours, or if it is pointing toward you, use this technique to wrap around their blade with a swiveling motion to send it out of alignment, and possibly out of their hands. With enough skill, you'll be able to pull your opponent's saber in like an object falling into orbit around a black hole.

Execution:

As your opponent attempts a stabbing attack, or if they have applied pressure against your blade...

1.   Breathe in. Return slight pressure against your opponent's blade.

2.   While maintaining contact with the middle-third of your blade, quickly hover your blade's tip over the top of your opponent's saber and underneath it (as if you were drawing a spiral-shape in the air with the tip).

3.   Continue this motion until you have found a direction in which your opponent's grip is weak (usually diagonally upward or straight downward). With a strong and jarring flick of your saber, send their blade in that direction.

4.   Return with a counter-attack (if possible), then return to the Ready Stance.

Checking Your Form: A great deal of power in this technique comes from maintaining good posture, and by keeping your arms close to your body. Be careful to maintain a tight grip on your hilt to keep this parry from back-firing. Ideally, when your opponent's saber is launched upward or downward, you will land a strike on them just before they can recover. While practicing, try to master flinging the opponent's saber in the same direction each time.

Mastery Code: YY5HK4T

Further Study: This technique is comparable to "*Makiotoshi*" and "*Makiage*" in kendo.

Form 1 Basic Low Parry

Summary: In this lesson, you'll review a near-instinctive low guard that will protect your legs from most attacks. Simply point your saber downward while twisting your body to face your opponent directly. Picture the first steps in cutting a circle in the floor around you, and you'll have an idea of what to do.

Execution:

As your opponent swings their saber downward to attempt a strike on your legs...

1. Slice your blade straight down, and off to one side as needed, to intercept the low attack (as if executing a putt in golf). Keep the tip a few inches from the ground and the pommel of your hilt a few inches from your stomach.

2. Twist your body slightly and/or take small steps so that you continue to face your opponent straight on.

3. Return with a counter-attack (if possible), then return to the Ready Stance.

Checking Your Form: It is a common mistake to bring your saber close in to your body, but that leaves you less protected, not more so. Keep your blade as far from your body as usual. If the attack comes from the side, you should still slice the blade straight down, and then sweep off to the side, keeping the tip consistently just a few inches off the ground. Maintain the home position with your feet as much as possible, making only the smallest of adjustments to your stance as needed. Alternate the leg you are protecting in your practices.

Mastery Code: USQCGDN

Further Study: This technique is comparable to the "Low *Daijyoudan* Guard" in kenjutsu.

Form 1 Basic Outside Arm Parry

Summary: A simple and near-instinctive defense, this technique can be used against many different attacks. In this lesson, you will be protecting yourself from an attack to your right side, but this technique works even better against attacks to your left side. As a saber's blade draws near to you, slap it away. Experts may even knock a saber from an opponent's hands in the process. Imagine how a disgusted royal ruler may swat at the side of the face of a subordinate, and you'll have the right idea.

Execution:

As your opponent attempts a downward strike to your arm or side...

1. Spring your saber blade upward in a curved line, swerving toward your opponent's blade, then up and away.

2. Twist (or "roll") your blade slightly away from the other blade when making contact to avoid it being manipulated in the process. (This should knock your opponent's blade away, usually diagonally upward.)

3. Return with a counter-attack (if possible) and assume the Ready Stance.

Checking Your Form: Always strive to be the first to strike. The idea here is to not hit the other blade very hard, but chaotically misdirect the other blade long enough for you to respond with a counter-attack. The overall motion of this technique should come from a snapping motion from your wrists in unison. Keep your upper arms and shoulders relaxed. Advanced students will keep an eye on where their opponent's left fingers are pointing, and attempt to sharply knock the other's hilt in that direction, dislodging their opponent's grip.

Practice this technique with a follow-up of an attack to a different target zone with each set.

Mastery Code: T6MKTSM

Further Study: This technique is comparable to *"Harai Waza"* in kendo and "The Slapping Parry" technique as found in The *Water Scroll* of Musashi's *Book of Five Rings.*

Form 1 Basic Inside Arm Parry

Summary: Another favorite of the RSA's founders, this intimidating parry involves "catching" an opponent's blade, and then walking into an opponent, applying pressure on them to retreat.

Execution:

As your opponent attempts a diagonal strike to your left arm...

1. Match your opponent's movements by chambering your hilt into your right shoulder and swinging your right foot back.

2. Breathe in. Before your opponent can complete their swing, interrupt their movement by stepping forward with your right foot and "catching" their blade with yours. (Maintain pressure against your opponent as if your blades were "glued" together.)

3. As you slowly breathe out, slide your left foot up and slide your right foot forward again. This should place you uncomfortably close to your opponent, forcing them to step back. (If you are not able to force your opponent to step back, counter-attacking their legs with a technique such as the Smuggler would be wise.)

4. Return to the Ready Stance.

Checking Your Form: Especially while applying pressure against your opponent's blade, keep your saber's hilt above theirs and flex your arms. The real strength of your defense will not come from your arms, but from your core and legs. If needed to close the distance, you can use regular Walking Step. Avoid the temptation to push your arms forward or to reach out with your hands. Rather, let your feet close the distance. While practicing, try to take large steps forward to compensate for the lack of resistance against your blade.

Mastery Code: R3LF6H7

Further Study: This technique utilizes the "Chambered *Hassou* guard" in kenjutsu and the "Body of the Short-Armed Monkey" and "Gluing" techniques from the *Water Scroll* of Musashi's *Book of Five Rings*.

Form 1 Basic Outside Flank Parry

Summary: This modest (yet effective) defense can be mastered almost as quickly as it is learned. In fact, if you are training young children, they will be able to get a lot of use out of this one lesson. It utilizes the protection that automatically comes from the Ready Position. With a focus on minimal effort, it ensures that any direct attack to your sides, arms, chest, or core is quickly thwarted. This is a perfect lesson for beginners, yet be careful not to rely on it as a crutch, as there are many much better ripostes to learn later.

Execution:

As your opponent attempts to strike you from the side...

1. Maintain a solid footing, tighten your grip, and keep your saber vertical.

2. Twist your torso to the side of the attack and push your saber forward (not inward) a moderate distance to deflect your opponent's saber away.

3. Continue outward in a circular motion (as if you were stirring a giant bowl of soup) then inward to return to the Ready Stance.

Checking Your Form: Rather than create a barrier to stop your opponent's horizontal swing, your parry should match your opponent's speed as if to attempt to "clap" blades together. Only then will you have a good chance of deflecting the attack. Try to keep the tip of the blade either skyward or tilted slightly toward your opponent's head as you execute all steps. The limit of how far your saber should be held away from your stomach is three-quarters of your fully-extended arm length.

Mastery Code: U9D7D4D

Further Study: This technique is comparable to the *motodachi's* role in an *"Uchikomi Geiko"* in which maneuvers such as *"Migi-Dou-uchi"* or *"Gyaku-Dou-uchi"* are being practiced in kendo.

Form 1 Basic Inside Flank Parry

Summary: It can be hazardous to remain in contact with an opponent's blade. This parry frees you from such a conflict, while also misdirecting your opponent's blade. Sharply slide your saber up the side of your opponent's with a snap, directing the tip of their blade off at an odd angle. The motion should be controlled and precise, like pulling back on a flight-control-stick in the cockpit as you pilot a craft upward. This technique also allows for some flexibility, as you are in control of which direction to spin your saber.

Execution:

As your opponent applies pressure against your blade (in a vertical position) in preparation for an attack, or after you have blocked against a flank attack...

1. Breathe in. Briefly maintain contact between the blades.

2. Slide the middle third of your blade up the side of your opponent's blade (building pressure) then release all pressure with a "snap," whipping the tip of the opponent's blade away.

3. Step diagonally forward with your right foot and continue the upward motion of your saber. Stir the tip your saber in a small circle (in the direction of your choice) above your head with its emitter just above your eyes.

4. Catch your left foot up to your right. Continue with your saber's momentum and swing down on your opponent's right shoulder. (If they are wearing a helmet, swing down on the top of it.) Breathe out.

5. Step back with your left and return to the Ready Stance.

Checking Your Form: The slide up, deflection, and downward strike of your saber should all be done in one fluid move. When the downward strike is made, be sure that your body is facing your target square on. When practicing, imagine starting this technique in different instances such as while defending your left flank, when defending your high target zone, when your opponent is applying pressure to your blade, and so forth.

Mastery Code: DPB4KUY

Further Study: This maneuver is comparable to the "*Tsuki-Suriage-Men*" and "*Men-Suriage-Men*" techniques in kendo.

Lesson: 28 - Temperate World Sequence

Form 1 Basic Partner Drills

Summary: For this drill, you will need a partner of equal or higher skill. (If such a partner cannot be found online or via the Rogue Saber Academy's resources, it would be prudent to train a friend or family member up to your level of expertise.) These partner drills will test your mastery of all basic attacks and parries. Give yourself and your partner plenty of room, preferably in an outdoor location. Before you begin, decide who will be "Partner A" and who will be "Partner B." Practice each movement slowly at first, alternating who will attack and who will defend, as many times as needed. The attacking partner should attempt to land a successful strike, each and every time. Likewise, the defending partner should always attempt a successful parry. It is important that Partner B only begins moving after Partner A has started their attack. When you are both comfortable with each technique, switch roles and take turns performing successful parries at regular dueling speed. Each drill is completed when you have both successfully demonstrated the particular parry five times. It is useful to count each successful parry, one right after the other, "One, one... Two, two... Three, three... etc." After you and your partner have done this for each of the following drills, you may both consider this lesson mastered.

Mindset: While completing the following drills, picture yourself as a student of an ancient order, training with other students on a lush green world of forests, mountains, and oceans. This particular location was chosen as a place to meditate on the mysterious forces of the universe. Be patient with your fellow student, as it may take more than one training session to complete every drill.

Execution:

Begin in the Attentive Stance, facing each other as if about to engage in an official spar or duel. Bow to your drill partner, and salute them with your signature flourish. Activate your saber and transition into the Ready Stance.

1. Partner A will initiate the first drill, attempting to land a strike with the **Knight's Strike** technique on Partner B. Partner B will attempt to prevent the strike with a parry, using the **Evader**. If Partner B was successful, the roles are switched, and Partner B will attack while Partner A defends, using the same techniques. Continue following this pattern until both partners have successfully defended with this technique five times, and then move on to the next drill. (Follow this pattern for all partner drills.)

2. Partner A attacks with the **Plasma Stab**, and Partner B defends with the **Deflector Shield**.

3. Partner A attacks with the **Pitfall** and Partner B defends with the **Gravity Well**.

4. Partner A attacks with the **Smuggler** and Partner B defends with the **Floor Escape**.

5. Partner A attacks with the **Hand Slice** and Partner B defends with the **Royal Rap**.

6. Partner A attacks with the **Clone Cutter** and Partner B defends with the **Rancor Rush**.

7. Partner A attacks with the **Hut Slap** and Partner B defends with the **All Too Easy**.

8. Partner A attacks with the **Crystal Mine** and Partner B defends with the **Pilot**.

9. Both partners deactivate their sabers and complete the drill with a handshake.

Mastery Code: UWNCA8D

Further Study: This partner drill is comparable to "*Kata Geiko*" paired training in kenjutsu and "*Yskudoku Geiko*" in kendo.

Intermediate Techniques

In order to master this lesson, simply make sure that you understand its contents so that you have a good idea of what to expect in the lessons to come.

The second third of the techniques in this manual are classified as "Intermediate." It is strongly recommended that all students become extensively familiar with these lessons before moving on to any of the advanced techniques. By the time you've reached this lesson, you would have ideally participated in at least one to five spars, duels, or tournaments, in which you and your opponent(s) are not simply practicing, but are attempting to best each other at full dueling speed. Hopefully by now, you've also established a routine in which you can participate in spars, engage in meditations, exercise daily, learn new lessons, and get in plenty of daily practice.

Students of the RSA would have typically reached the rank of "Novice" in the Rogue Order before completing this lesson. If you belong to a club or dojo, check with your instructor to see if you are deemed ready to move on in their program before studying the intermediate techniques.

Intermediate Attacks:

The next lessons you will come across are "Indirect Attacks." These are techniques that require more skill than the previous ones, and also include two or more key steps in execution. You will begin to attack in different phases of the match, and not always as a proactive attacker. Rather than go directly for your target, you will make a preparatory action, often to misdirect the attention of your opponent, or to adjust yourself in order to be in a better position to strike. Sometimes, you will rely on an action from your opponent as a signal to start off a particular maneuver, allowing them to make the first move. This is the "preemption from a state of waiting." When that happens, you'll either avoid the attack or respond aggressively, changing the pace of the match. If your first attempt to strike is thwarted, strike again immediately when your opponent is relaxing. Indirect attacks still focus on making one strike and one point, but they are good introductory techniques as you prepare for composite attacks to come.

At this point in your training, there is a greater emphasis on your own body language. Always be aware of what you are telegraphing to your opponent, and be deliberate in what you are communicating. These lessons will also introduce you to contingency plans, or alternate actions depending on how your opponent reacts in certain situations. They can be utilized in all stages of a duel, and add to your versatility and adaptability.

As you progress through these lessons, more is expected of your performance. Always keep your combat saber moving and movements flowing. Recognize that your attack does not depend just on what you want to execute but also the position of your opponent. Therefore, a match is like a dance, with movements of both parties playing essential roles. You should not let yourself be surprised by your opponent, because you are reading their actions so carefully. Through all your preparatory actions, always keep the end goal, the strike, in mind.

As attacks get more complicated, you may be tempted to skip steps or adjust each lesson to suit what is comfortable to you. A student must avoid this. It is important that you learn a technique and master it with technical perfection long before making it your own.

Intermediate Ripostes:

Now that you have learned how to protect yourself, you are ready to move on to learn counter-attacks. Ripostes can be thought of as 10% reactive and 90% proactive. It helps to adopt the mindset that you are always the aggressor, and do not make any defensive movement. Rather, you only interrupt an opponent's attack with your superior attack. This is how a proper riposte works. Of course, if your opponent is making frivolous or excessive movements, allow them to do so. If you allow your opponent to make wasteful movements, it actually goes to your advantage. Yet if you are stuck in the mindset that you are always trying to thwart your opponent's advances, you have already lost. Keep yourself on your "forward foot," so to speak. Stop any attempt of making a strike against you at its outset. In the moment your opponent thinks about attacking you, prevent them from following through, and then rebound with your own dedicated strike while they are caught off guard. This is in the Japanese tradition of "Killing the technique," or "*Waza wo korsu*,"in which a duelist focuses on gaining the upper hand by breaking the flow of an opponent's intended attack, and returning with an attack of one's own.

Mastery Code: SSPJBLB

Further Study: On techniques like these, feel free to look up the "Three Preemptions" and "Holding Down the Pillow" in the Fire Scroll, as well as "On the Teaching of Having a Position Without a Position" and "The Rhythm of the Second Spring" in the *Water Scroll*, in Musashi's *Book of Five Rings*. In addition, you can look into "*Go-no-sen*," "*Oji waza*," and "*Hikibana Waza*" in kendo.

Form 1 Intermediate High Attack

Summary: Is your opponent parrying all of your attacks? The solution may be to perform a "feint" on one side, and strike on the other. There are a few techniques in this manual that utilize this approach, but none are as simple as this devastatingly useful maneuver. Swing your saber up and swing down diagonally to the side of the neck of your opponent to draw your opponent's saber away, then swing it back over your head with a surprise attack to the other side. Consider the cunning bounty hunter, and the bold tactics needed to defeat them before they defeat you.

Execution:

1. Assume the Ready Stance.

2. Breathe in. Lift your saber straight up, elbows pointing away from the face. Keep lifting the saber up until the blade tip is pointing straight behind you and your hilt is directly over your head.

3. Slide your right foot forward and to the right, followed quickly by your left as you swivel your saber overhead and diagonally down, aiming for the close side of the neck (without too much force and with safety in mind). Breathe out.

4. Feint away by reversing the motion, breathe in and quickly step back with your left foot, then right, raising your saber again over your head.

5. Immediately (before your opponent can prepare for your follow-up attack) step forward, with your left foot, to the other side of your opponent and perform the mirror-image

of your last technique, targeting the other side of the neck. Breathe out.

6. If this strike is unsuccessful, and the original side of the neck is unprotected, switch to target the other side again. Otherwise, return to the Ready Stance.

Checking Your Form: If you can anticipate a parry from your opponent on one side, feel free to redirect your attack to the other side instantaneously. As you can imagine, all steps in this technique can be mirrored to target a different side as needed. In any case, restraint and caution should be exercise when targeting the neck area, for safety. Try not to swing your saber too far out so that it is swung horizontally like a baseball bat. Rather, your swing should be diagonal from above your head in order to strike the neck between 45° and 90°. Keep your shoulders down throughout each movement.

Mastery Code: NC2JVDK

Further Study: This technique utilizes the "*Daijyoudan* stance" and the "*Ichimonji Men Giri*" in kenjutsu.

Form 1 Intermediate Chest Attack

Summary: Will your opponent take the bait? While a true student of kendo would never dream of being deceptive in a duel, this technique invites your opponent to strike high, only to be chopped across the torso with a surprise attack. Point your saber backward and rest your hilt on your right hip. When your opponent raises their saber, rush forward with a horizontal slice to the chest.

Execution:

1. Assume the Ready Stance.

2. Drop your saber down and point it behind you and toward the ground on your right side. While keeping both hands on the hilt, rest the hilt on your right hip.

3. Breathe in. Take a large step toward your opponent with your left foot to close the distance between you. Lean forward and turn your body so that your head and torso is exposed to a high attack. (This will also conceal your saber from the view of your opponent.)

4. Step to the side or toward your opponent as needed to elicit a response while keeping your left foot ahead of your right.

5. As soon as your opponent raises their saber upward in order to attack your high target zone, chest, or arms, take a large step with your right foot to the left side of them (from your perspective).

6. Breathe out. Simultaneously while stepping, swing your saber forward and upward, slicing them just under their arms.

7. Pull your saber horizontally (cutting the chest) as you take another large step with your left foot past your opponent.

8. Pivot both feet in order to turn your body and face your opponent again in the Ready Stance.

Checking Your Form: Maintain control of your breathing, and add pressure to each breath by flexing your core. Be ready to react to your opponent's motions with a predetermined reflex in mind, so that you lose no time planning each step in the heat of the moment. Aim your strike lower, closer to the stomach, against female opponents. If more steps are needed to get close enough to your opponent, use Primed Step.

Mastery Code: LLWAMHN

Further Study: This technique utilizes the "Counter from a *Waki Gamae* stance" and "*Migi Ichimonji Giri*" in kenjutsu.

Form 1 Intermediate Core Attack

Summary: A stylistic move near-and-dear to the hearts of master duelists is this technique that mimics the motion of drawing a sword out of a sheath on the hip and slicing an opponent from their right hip to their left shoulder in one dramatic movement. This is a good attack for getting you out of a predictable pattern in the eyes of an opponent and for changing the pace of a duel in your favor.

Execution:

1. Assume the Ready Stance.

2. Drop your saber down and point it behind you and toward the ground on your left side. While keeping both hands awkwardly crossed on the hilt, rest the hilt on your left hip. Breathe in.

3. Take a small step forward or back, in order to keep in proper striking distance. Release your left hand from the hilt and keep it against your hip (as if holding a scabbard back).

4. Without warning, lunge forward with your right foot while swinging your saber with your right hand diagonally up and to your right. Target your opponent's stomach so that it is grazed with the tip of your saber. (For safety reasons, do not strike your opponent just below their sternum. Rather, "enter" at their right hip and "exit" near the lower edge of their left ribs.) Breathe out.

5. Pull your saber and right foot back into the Ready Position.

Checking Your Form: As you pull your saber forward, draw your left hand back at the same time, as if pulling its scabbard back. When swinging your saber upward, do not twist your body. Instead, keep your chest facing perfectly ahead of you. Practice this technique several times against a stationary object (such as a chair) in order to familiarize yourself with exactly how far you will need to stand from your opponent in order to graze their core with your saber, while holding it with just one hand. Keep your movements rigid, clean, and concise. For example, stop your saber dead, briefly freezing it in the air just after it passes your opponent's left flank, with your right arm fully extended after the cut.

Mastery Code: 5CXTMVU

Further Study: This technique utilizes the "Reverse *Waki Gamae* Stance," "*Hidari Joho Giri*," and the "*Iai*" strike in kenjutsu, and is comparable to the "*Battou*" technique in iaido.

Form 1 Intermediate Low Attack

Summary: Size matters not, but this technique does require smooth timing and flexibility. If your opponent is overly aggressive, this is a good technique to use as an alternative to retreating backward. You'll learn how to use a new level to your advantage as your opponent awkwardly tries to guard against a low swing. Sink into a low squat while keeping your blade up to protect you, swing the blade to slice against the leg of your opponent, then rise back up, cutting upward.

Execution:

1. Assume the Ready Stance.

2. Use the Primer Step in small ways to close the distance between you and your opponent. Bring yourself within striking distance.

3. Breathe in. Lift your blade upward and point it back (with your saber's emitter above your forehead) so that it is ready to block an attack from your opponent down on your head, shoulders, chest, or arms.

4. Turn your back foot to the left and take a step outward so that your feet are perpendicular (not parallel) to each other. (How far to the back left should you step? It all depends on how wide you need your stance to be in order to squat down properly.)

5. Sink your body down, keeping a straight back. Lower your hips as far as you can comfortably go while allowing yourself an easy recovery. Keep the motion controlled while being easy on the knees.

6. While your left hand keeps the base of your hilt centered with your body, your right hand whips the tip of your blade to the right, down, and upward (in a "backward J" movement), hitting your opponent's left leg at an upward angle. (An additional thrust from the left hand forward may be needed to reach the opponent.) Breathe out.

7. Keep your saber against the leg of your opponent, and slide it up the side of their body as you rise straight up until it reaches their arm. You can try a strike to your opponent's flank on the way up if you choose. (If you do manage to strike the arm, you may be granted a second point. Alternatively, if your low attack was thwarted, your second attempt may be successful.)

8. Pull your saber back and return to the Ready Stance.

Checking Your Form: Keep your neck and shoulders relaxed. As you sink into a squatting position, your opponent will most likely step back. Therefore, a quick transition and an extended reach with your saber can help secure a point. As you swing your saber to the side, center your weight onto your right toes to avoid throwing yourself off balance. Do not allow your knees to bend in front of your toes, and do not strike your opponent on the knee. Rather, sit your body further back and target a large muscle on your opponent's leg.

Mastery Code: YEHY7YD

Further Study: This technique is comparable to the "*Gyaku-Dou*" strike in kendo and "*Kiri age*" maneuvers in kenjutsu.

Form 1 Intermediate Outside Arm Attack

Summary: You have learned three one-handed techniques utilizing your right hand, but in this lesson, you'll see what your left hand can do in a pinch. An inversion of the Pitfall technique, you will slide down the outside edge of your opponent's blade and extend your left hand forward to chop down on their right wrist.

Execution:

1. Assume the Ready Stance.

2. Breathe in. If needed, swing your blade around your opponent's saber so that it rests on the left side of your opponent's blade (from your perspective).

3. Let go of your saber with your right hand, and bring your right hand toward your chest with an open outward-facing palm.

4. Step forward with your left foot, twisting your body to the side and extending your left hand forward. Slide down the side of your opponent's blade (without necessarily making any contact) in order to strike their right wrist.

5. Cut your saber straight back as you bring your left foot back into the Ready Stance.

Checking Your Form: As with most techniques, this should be practiced so that it can be executed in one swift stroke. The left step forward need not be a large one, as long as the left arm is fully extended. Rather than "hugging" your opponent's saber, it is more effective to launch your saber forward, like a chameleon's tongue catching a fly. Strength and precision will be added to your thrust if you twist your hilt clockwise, just as you would twist a punch with your left hand in karate.

Mastery Code: RW825AC

Further Study: This technique is comparable to the *"Katatetsuki"* strike and the *"Degote"* strike in kendo.

Form 1 Intermediate Inside Arm Attack

Summary: The feint is a key element in modern European fencing. Performing a feint is simple enough: As you move to strike one target, you quickly change targets in order to stay one step ahead of your opponent's defenses. However, in kendo, an attempt to mislead or deceive an opponent is seen as counter to the honorable spirit of the samurai. Therefore, any technique approaching a feint must be subtle and rely far more on your opponent's poor assumptions (rather than your misdirection). In this technique, you will strike the underside of your opponent's left wrist by way of a movement similar to the Hand Slice technique that you have previously mastered. However, rather than hitting the right wrist, you will curve your saber under the hands and cut upward to the left arm. The tip of your blade should spiral into its target, like a homing torpedo.

Execution:

1. Assume the Ready Stance.

2. Breathe in. Take a shorter-than-usual step forward (and slightly to your left) with your right foot.

3. Lift your saber straight up, elbows pointing just a few degrees off from directly forward. Only lift the saber far enough so that the hilt is just above your eyes. Twist on your right foot so that your body is facing your opponent's right forearm.

4. As you catch your left foot up, slice your saber downward in a straight and controlled vertical line so that it falls just past the edge of your opponent's right arm.

5. Continue the motion without slowing, creating a hook shape under your opponent's fingers and saber hilt. Step with your right foot to the right, leaving you in a wide stance.

6. Strike your opponent's left wrist on the upswing. Breathe out.

7. Draw your saber upward and back (as if slicing through the forearm). Bring your left foot sideways into the home position.

8. Return to the Ready Stance.

Checking Your Form: While your blade is coming down, make sure that your arms remain tight against your body and that you squeeze the hilt tightly to redirect its motion. Your step to the right should be swift and only come after your opponent's blade has moved to counter an attack to their right wrist. The upward strike should turn your opponent's saber even further away from you, granting you plenty of time to put up your guard.

Mastery Code: VBX4MLQ

Further Study: This technique references "Good *Seme*" methods, and is comparable to "*Gyaku-Kote-uchi*" and "*Nuki waza*" in kendo.

Form 1 Intermediate Outside Flank Attack

Summary: Can you run to one side of your opponent but swing your saber to attack their other side? It is a risky, yet valuable maneuver. (The Spice Run is similar to the Maul technique, but attacks from the other side.) This is a surprise attack, best done when an opponent's arms are up and away from their body. In a motion like swinging a pickaxe downward to strike rock (or something less innocuous), you'll raise your saber high and make a C shape down to strike the outside flank of your opponent, and then slice horizontally while making a quick getaway past their inside flank.

Execution:

1. Assume the Ready Stance. Target your opponent's right flank when it is exposed.

2. Breathe in. Take two quick walking steps to the right side of your opponent (from your perspective). Raise your saber (only so high that the emitter of your saber is just in front of your face).

3. Swing your saber downward to your left, making a C shape. Make contact against your opponent's outside flank with the last third or middle third of your blade. Breathe out.

4. Upon making contact, let go of your saber with your left hand. Continue to run past your opponent, allowing your blade to drag along your opponent's core region, horizontally cutting as you continue to step forward. (Rather than pulling or swinging your blade free with your hands, let it simply follow your body's motion.)

5. Once your saber is free of your opponent, suspend your saber in place, pivot on your feet, and center your body around your saber. Return to the Ready Stance.

Checking Your Form: When making contact with your opponent's right side, twist your hands as if you were making a horizontal cut, rather than just tapping the side of your blade against their side. Before making the attack, be sure to have both your footwork and your hand work in mind.

Mastery Code: A5XC7Q3

Further Study: This technique is comparable to the "*Migi-dou-uchi*" in kendo and "*Hidari Ichimonji Kiri*" in kenjutsu.

Form 1 Intermediate Inside Flank Attack

Summary: In a move similar to the overhead swivel of the Bounty Hunter technique (yet with less footwork), you will target one side of the opponent, and then the other, in a rapid-switching flurry until gaining purchase. Your saber may not be able to deflect bolts of plasma, but if it could, this technique would come in handy.

Execution:

1. Assume the Ready Stance.

2. Breathe in. Lift your saber straight up, elbows pointing away from the face. Keep lifting the saber up until the blade tip is pointing straight behind you and your hilt is directly over your head.

3. Take a medium-sized step forward with your right foot, followed quickly by your left as you swivel your saber overhead and diagonally down, aiming for your opponent's left flank. Breathe out.

4. If the strike was unsuccessful, breathe in. Without moving your feet, raise your saber again over your head.

5. Immediately (before your opponent can prepare for your follow-up attack) perform the mirror-image of your last technique, targeting their right flank. Breathe out.

6. If this strike is unsuccessful, switch to target the other side again. Repeat this process quickly until you have landed a strike, or until your opponent has begun to anticipate your movements.

7. Step both feet back, starting with your left, and return to the Ready Stance.

Checking Your Form: If you can anticipate a parry from your opponent on one side, feel free to redirect your attack to the other side instantaneously as part of a feint. Never lose sense of where your opponent's blade is moving, and be flexible enough to adjust your line of attack if needed at any moment.

Mastery Code: A73KT32

Further Study: This technique utilizes the *"Daijyoudan* stance" in kenjutsu. It is also comparable to *"Dou-Uchi"* and *"Renzoku waza"* in kendo.

Form 1 Intermediate Attack Pattern Drill

Summary: You are now ready to demonstrate your proficiency utilizing the intermediate attacks you have learned. You do not need a partner for this drill, but you are encouraged to imagine a scenario in which you are competing for the chance to continue your learning against a space hangar filled with other students. The students are all of your same skill level, and all of your sabers have been powered down to stun on contact, rather than cut. While the others are backed against the walls of the hangar, you boldly step out into the center. Perform each technique crisply, with perfect form, and with smooth transitions. In the instructions below, you will again be directed to follow Clock Position orientation. Give yourself plenty of room, preferably outdoors. Start out by performing each technique and transition slowly, and then work up to doing it at full dueling speed. Once you can complete this entire drill from memory, without additional pausing or making a mistake, you will have proven to yourself (as well as to the imagined judges) that you are ready to continue on with your training.

Execution:

1. Begin in the **Attentive Stance**, facing 12:00, and standing in the center point of your practice space. Bow to your first rival student (standing at 12:00), activate your saber, and salute with your signature flourish.

2. Transition into the **Ready Stance**. Picture your rivals all igniting their sabers as well.

3. Take one (primed) step forward with each foot, and pause. A brief moment passes as you and the first student face each other, just out of striking distance.

4. Slide your right foot forward and a little to the right, and perform the **Bounty Hunter**. Your first attempt to strike the first student's neck fails as she steps back. Aggressively pursue with your left foot forward (with Walking Step) and land a strike on the other side of her neck, sending her stunned to the ground.

5. You hear the hum of the saber wielded by the second student behind you. Pivot on both feet to turn your body to the right and back, keeping your saber pointed up and forward. Face 6:00 in the Ready Stance, yet with your feet wider apart than usual.

6. Your quick turn surprises the second student, and he takes a large step back, almost running into a third student, who steps back in turn, keeping an eye on you. Step toward 6:00 with your left foot and chamber your saber on your right hip with its blade pointing backward.

7. As the second student summons his courage and attempts an attack on your head, you step toward 5:00 (slightly to your left) with your left foot, then right, executing the **Maul**. Continue your swing after hitting the second student's chest, bringing your saber all the way around to your left hip, chambering it there. (Your right foot should be slightly ahead of your left.)

8. The second student collapses as the third advances head-on toward you and attempts a strike to the left side of your neck. Take a large right step forward (lowering and protecting your neck and head in the process while maintaining good posture) to perform the **Quick Draw**. As their blade swings over your head, your blade's tip buzzes across their core, and they fall back.

9. While the remaining students have kept their distance from you, sparring amongst themselves, one especially tall and

strong student lumbers toward you from 11:00 (directly behind you as you face 5:00). Immediately raise your saber over your head to protect against a strike from high above. Pivot on both feet again to face the large fourth student, turning to the left.

10. Step your right foot forward and your left foot out at a perpendicular angle. As the fourth student attempts a strike to your right arm, you squat down (allowing their saber to pass overhead and to your left) and execute the **Do or Do Not**.

11. As you strike the fourth student's left leg, flank, and left arm, you realize that their size and strength grants them greater-than-average resistance to the stunning effects of your saber. Pull back into the Ready Stance. The fourth student then attempts to knock your saber to your right, so you lean back and pull your saber back so that its blade almost grazes your face. Once your saber is on the left side of theirs, perform the **Force Push**, targeting the fourth student's left arm.

12. Once you have returned to the Ready Stance, immediately perform the **Torpedo**, finally overwhelming the fourth student, who collapses.

13. Using Walking Step, return to the center point, stepping over the stunned students, and assume the Ready Stance. Turn to face 9:00 where the last two remaining students have agreed to team up against you before dueling each other.

14. Take a large right step forward between the two of them, chambering your saber into your left shoulder. Pause for a moment, allowing them to make the first move.

15. All at once, they both charge toward you. You'll first attack the one on the right (from your perspective). Step toward 9:00 with your left, right, then left foot, using the **Spice Run** to down the fifth student then immediately turn to face 6:00, swinging your saber over your head, to assail the final student, who followed behind you, with the **Blaster Fire**.

16. Your first and second strikes are deflected by their saber, but you at last strike true onto the final student's left flank with the third attempt, sending her down.

17. Deactivate your saber. Spin it down and back to your left hip, held in place by your left hand. Pivot on both feet to again face the center point and take a few (walking) steps to return to it.

18. Turn to face 12:00 in the Attentive Stance.

19. Bow to the judges observing from above.

Mastery Code: H9ZXT9A

Further Study: This drill is comparable to "*Hitori Geiko*" and solo *kata* sequences in kendo, kenjutsu, and iaido.

Form 1 Intermediate High Riposte

Summary: Diagonal or horizontal attacks to your high target area can be intimidating. Yet with this maneuver, you will turn the tide of battle in your favor. Like a heavy blast door dropping shut, you will knock your opponent's saber down aggressively as you step forward and strike horizontally into their shoulder.

Execution:

As your opponent targets your head or neck with a horizontal or diagonal swing...

1. Breathe in and lift your saber's hilt straight up, at least to your eye level. Step your left foot diagonally back, away from the attack.

2. Breathe out sharply, and with great force, swing your saber down diagonally (between directly forward and directly to your side) to catch your opponent's saber with the middle third of your blade. Return your right foot to the home position.

3. Push off your left foot and step your right forward. Immediately twist your saber to cut inward. Target your opponent's shoulder (the one nearest your blade).

4. Horizontally strike into your opponent's shoulder and draw it backward (as if slicing deep into the arm).

5. Pull your right foot back into the Ready Stance.

Checking Your Form: Be careful not to waste any time between raising your saber and swinging it downward. The upward motion should be like the compressing of a spring, building tension. The downward motion should shoot out, releasing all that tension. Such a powerful crash against your opponent's blade may send it out of their hands. Make sure to strike your opponent's saber directly from above, and not from the side.

Mastery Code: H9ZXT9A

Further Study: This technique is comparable to "*Uchiotoshi Waza*" in general and the "*Men-Uchiotoshi-Men*" maneuver in kendo. It is also comparable to "The Crimson Foliage Hit" technique in the *Water Scroll* of Musashi's *Book of Five Rings*.

Form 1 Intermediate Chest Riposte

Summary: A tricky procedure (ideal for a slippery villain), this riposte will allow you to narrowly avoid a horizontal cut to the chest by stepping around your opponent's blade to the left. You'll then exact your revenge with a left-handed chop down to both of your opponent's wrists. This technique can be thought of as a side-on combination of the Evader and the Force Push.

Execution:

As your opponent swings their saber horizontally from your left to cut your chest...

1. Take a wide step directly to the left with your left foot. (This will set you just outside of the turning radius of your opponent's blade, which you should allow to swing past you.)

2. Follow your left foot with your right. Let go of your saber with your right hand, and bring your right hand toward your chest with an open palm.

3. (Optional Step: If you are not in range, lunge toward your opponent's hands with your left foot.)

4. Extend your saber with your left hand to strike down on your opponent's wrists with the last third of your blade.

5. Cut your saber straight back as you bring your left foot back into the Ready Stance.

Checking Your Form: When your opponent has their saber hidden behind them (such as when their hilt is resting on a hip), rely upon your opponent's shoulder movements to tell you when and where they will aim their strike. Do not underestimate the length of your opponent's saber when practicing on your own. Be sure to make your initial step wide, but not so wide that you compromise your stance. After some practice, your goal should be to step to the side and swing down with your left hand at the same time, even if your specific target (the outside arm) is not yet in range before you begin your riposte. If your opponent attacks from the opposite direction, all movements in this technique can be mirrored, although you would have less reach in the final blow.

Mastery Code: G43V9SH

Further Study: This technique is comparable to a counter against an "*Ichimonji*" cut from the "*Waki Gamea*" stance in kenjutsu.

Form 1 Intermediate Core Riposte

Summary: Would you like to stoke your reputation with the crowd? This is a riposte for duelists with style. It works well against stabbing attacks, horizontal swings, and most chest, core, or low attacks. With only your right hand on your saber, point it down and sweep it to the left. Follow your opponent's saber (or knock it to the side), then spin your saber over your head with both hands to land a satisfying strike on your opponent's left shoulder.

Execution:

If your opponent's blade's tip approaches your core or chest from your right...

1. Take a large step back with your right foot, backing your body out of range of the attack.

2. Bring your saber low so that your opponent's blade passes over it. Point your saber downward and let go of it with your left hand. Twist your wrist so that the hilt's pommel passes underneath your forearm, from the left side to the right.

3. Breathe in. Raise the hilt of your saber straight upward while keeping its tip pointed downward. (Your right palm should be facing to your right as your thumb points down.)

4. Follow the direction of your opponent's blade, pushing it if possible, in an upward spiral around your body.

5. Return your left hand to the saber as it spins over your head.

6. Once the tip of your saber is pointing behind you, take aim to your opponent's inside shoulder, in line with the right side of your body.

7. Step your right foot forward and swing your saber down in a clean slice to strike the shoulder. Breathe out.

8. Take a small step back with your left foot and bring your body back into the Ready Stance.

If your opponent's blade's tip approaches your core or chest from your left or head-on as a stab...

1. Breathe in. Point your saber downward and let go of it with your left hand. Twist your wrist so that the hilt's pommel passes underneath your forearm, from the left side to the right.

2. Raise the hilt of your saber straight upward while keeping its tip pointed downward. (Your right palm should be facing to your right as your thumb points down.)

3. Swing aggressively to the left to meet your opponent's blade and knock it aside. Continue the motion in an upward spiral around your body.

4. Return your left hand to the saber as it spins over your head.

5. Once the tip of your saber is pointing behind you, take aim to your opponent's inside shoulder, in line with the right side of your body.

6. Swing your saber down in a clean slice to strike the shoulder. Breathe out.

7. Take a small step back with your left foot and bring your body back into the Ready Stance.

Checking Your Form: Keep your shoulders relaxed and maintain good posture. Tighten your abdominal muscles during the technique in order to increase your speed and improve your balance. After dropping your left hand, you need only raise your right hand so that the hilt of your saber is at about eye level. The success of this riposte does not rely on the strength of the block (which is weak as it is supported with only one hand), but with the speed and coordination of your movements.

Mastery Code: 97JWX38

Further Study: This technique is comparable to an "Inward Downward Block" utilizing the *"Migi Kesa Giri"* in kenjutsu.

Form 1 Intermediate Low Riposte

Summary: In this cerebral sport, it is easy to overthink one's movements and strategy. A skilled duelist, however, acts without an extra thought, like a trained soldier when given a command. If your opponent has assumed a low-level position (as seen in the Do or Do Not technique), circle around the right side of your opponent with three quick steps, then land an attack on either their right or left flank.

Execution:

As your opponent drops down to target your legs...

1. Immediately take three quick steps in Walking Step, circling around the right side of your opponent. Breathe in while raising your saber so that its emitter reaches your eye level. (Your last step should end with you facing the back of your opponent's torso.)

2. As your opponent stands, rolls, turns, or moves their saber to protect against your strike, eye which of their sides is more exposed.

3. Swing your saber straight down then swerve it to one side in a hooking-motion so that it intercepts their exposed flank horizontally. Breathe out.

4. Return to the Ready Stance.

Checking Your Form: Even though your opponent has squatted down or knelt on the ground, you should still keep excellent posture in preparation for any surprises. Raise your saber exactly straight and in line with the center of your body above you. The first half of your swing down should be perfectly vertical as well.

Mastery Code: VZ7ZC9K

Further Study: This technique is comparable to the "*Nuki Waza*," "*Ayumi ashi*," and the low swing of "*Joge buri*" in kendo.

Form 1 Intermediate Outside Arm Riposte

Summary: Do you want to save your hands from getting chopped? This technique pulls them up and out of harm's way (like those of a frozen smuggler) and immediately converts the motion into a step to the side and downward strike onto the inside wrist of your opponent. This is a technique for the fast thinker, and takes advantage of the perfect distance to your target provided by your opponent. (It is similar to the Evader technique, but is tighter and quicker, and includes steps to the opposite side and attacks a different target.)

Execution:

As your opponent swings their saber downward to strike your wrists...

1. Breathe in. Lift your saber straight up, so that both hands are free from harm, and your left hand is hovering at eye level.

2. Take a substantial step diagonally forward and (mostly) to the left with your left foot.

3. As you bring your right foot back and to the right of your left (in a reverse home position), slice downward in a C shape onto the outside arm of your opponent (above the elbow) with the last third of your saber's blade. Breathe out.

4. Step your left foot back to return to the Ready Stance.

Checking Your Form: Practice lifting your blade straight up (and leaning slightly back above your head) and straight down while curving into the cut. While your blade is coming down, keep your wrists in line with your arms and make sure that your arms remain tight against your body. Squeeze the hilt tightly to slow and stop its motion.

Your final strike should be in line with the center line of your body as you squarely face your opponent's arm.

Mastery Code: EXFRRKQ

Further Study: This technique is comparable to the "*Kote-Nuki-Kote*" maneuver with the "*Hiraki ashi*" step in kendo.

Form 1 Intermediate Inside Arm Riposte

Summary: Are you looking for a real challenge? This riposte is not for the faint of heart. However, any practice dedicated to mastering it is well spent. Like skimming the surface of a battle station (while being pursued by enemies) to deal a fatal blow, this technique requires you to dive inside the striking range of your opponent. It is an advanced form of the Spice Run, with the added precursor of knocking your opponent's saber up and swinging your blade around theirs. Split your attack, and escape to opposite sides of your opponent as before. Strike their outside flank, and escape to the right.

Execution:

As the tip of your opponent's blade approaches your wrists...

1. Breathe in. Lower your saber and aim your saber's tip toward your opponent's hands, so that the blades are near parallel.

2. Once your opponent's saber draws near, knock it upward and slightly to the left. Continue for a brief moment to raise your saber.

3. While keeping your saber's hilt directly in front of your chest, swivel your blade around the tip of your opponent's blade. The middle third of your blade should leave the right side of your opponent's saber (from your perspective), draw near to your face, and off to the left.

4. Once your blade passes over to your left, take a large step diagonally forward and to the right with your right foot.

5. With walking steps, run past the side of your opponent while striking their outside flank.

6. Allow your saber to "drag" along their core as you hold it only with your right hand.

7. Once you are a safe distance away, face your opponent again in the Ready Stance.

Checking Your Form: When you swivel your saber around your opponent's, your left hand should remain locked in place. The swivel motion should be done completely with your right hand. Time your right foot's step so that it touches down when your saber is closest to your face. As you step with your right foot, don't forget to push off with your left. When you make the strike, your right thumb should be pointed outward as if you were chopping horizontally to the right.

Mastery Code: VYYU5MR

Further Study: This technique is comparable to "*Men-Kaeshi-Dou*" or "*Kote-Kaeshi-Dou*" in kendo.

Form 1 Intermediate Outside Flank Riposte

Summary: To target your flank, an opponent may charge to one side of you while their saber swings to the other. With this technique, you will be able to use their momentum to your advantage, protect your side, and meet their stomach with the side of your blade. Point your saber downward on your right side as you step back and turn your left side back. Spin your saber up and to the left in order to cut into your opponent's core as they rush by.

Execution:

As your opponent steps to your left side while their saber comes down on your right...

1. Breathe in. Take a wide arc-shaped step left and back with your left foot so that it lands perpendicular to your right foot. (Your left toes should be pointing to the left as your right toes point to your opponent.)

2. Lift your right hand to your eye level and keep it hovering in place while your left hand raises higher, dropping the tip of the saber down to guard your outside flank. Simultaneously, twist your body sideways to aim your right shoulder at your opponent.

3. Once your opponent's blade hits against yours (as if to "spring the trap") use your left hand to push the pommel of your hilt away from your face and down to a fist's distance from your stomach. At the same time, extend your right hand forward. As you spin your saber, its tip should travel in a diagonal path from behind you and to the right in a slice to meet your opponent's core in front of you and to the left. Breathe out.

4. Take a large step back and away from your opponent with your left foot, followed by a small step with your right to return to the Ready Stance.

Checking Your Form: Tighten your abdominal muscles while you move your saber to help with your posture. When you point your saber downward to protect your side, point the tip away from your feet slightly so that the saber is not perfectly vertical. Keep your right hand far enough from your face so that your blade does not threaten the back of your head as you swing it diagonally. Avoid holding your saber too close to your body while blocking or striking.

Mastery Code: 3J4K962

Further Study: This technique is comparable to *"Dou-Kaeshi-Dou"* and *"Dou-Kaeshi-Men"* in kendo.

Form 1 Intermediate Inside Flank Riposte

Summary: Is your opponent attempting to disarm you, or assail you with repeated attacks to your sides? Make them regret it by knocking their saber aside and raining down this caustic counter-attack. If your opponent attacks from your right, knock their saber to your right, stir your blade overhead, and attack their inside wrist. If they attack from your left, knock their saber to your left, stir your saber, and attack their outside wrist. (Although sharing similarities with the Trench Run, this maneuver requires much less risk, calls for you to raise your saber higher to go over, not around, their blade, and does not send you and your saber to different sides of your opponent.)

Execution:

As your opponent swings their saber in an attempt to strike your RIGHT (outside) wrist or flank...

1. Breathe in. As if drawing an S shape in the air (starting with the lowest point), knock their blade to your right and raise your saber so that its emitter is just in front of your face.

2. Take a small step to the right with your right foot so that you face your opponent's inside wrist directly.

3. Continue with the momentum from your parry and "stir" the tip of your blade in the air (finishing the top portion of the S) over to the other side of your opponent's saber.

4. As your left foot takes its place beside your right, whip the last third of your blade down, targeting and hitting your opponent on the wrist that is nearest to you. Breathe out.

5. Stand your ground in the Ready Stance.

As your opponent swings their saber in an attempt to strike your LEFT (inside) wrist or flank...

1. Breathe in. As if drawing a curved Z shape in the air (starting with the lowest point), knock their blade to your left and raise your saber so that its emitter is just in front of your face.

2. Take a small step to the left with your left foot so that you face your opponent's outside wrist directly.

3. Continue with the momentum from your parry and "stir" the tip of your blade in the air (finishing the top portion of the curved Z) over to the other side of your opponent's saber.

4. As your right foot takes its place beside your left, whip the last third of your blade down, targeting and hitting your opponent on the wrist that is nearest to you. Breathe out.

5. Stand your ground in the Ready Stance.

Checking Your Form: Keep your shoulders relaxed. When striking down on your opponent's wrist, be sure to face your body square onto your target, and extend your right arm as far as it will reach without compromising your posture. As you practice, perform both versions of this maneuver, one after another, and focus on landing a successful counter-attack each time, rather than stop after an effective parry.

Mastery Code: R2WBSH4

Further Study: This technique is comparable to the "*Kote-Kaeshi-Kote*" maneuver in kendo, and utilizes "*Hiki waza.*"

Lesson: 47 - Ice World Sequence

Form 1 Intermediate Partner Drills

Summary: As with the Basic Partner Drills, you will need a partner of equal or higher skill, and lots of space, to test your knowledge of all of the intermediate attacks and ripostes in this sequence. Decide who will be "Partner A" and who will be "Partner B" before starting. Practice each movement slowly at first, alternating who will attack and who will defend, as many times as needed. The attacking partner should attempt to land a successful strike, each and every time. At this level, the defending partner should always attempt a successful riposte (landing a successful counter-strike). It is important that Partner B only begins moving after Partner A has started their attack. When you are both comfortable with each technique, take turns performing successful ripostes at a regular dueling speed. When you have both successfully demonstrated the particular riposte five times (thus completing a drill), move on, until you've mastered the drills in total.

Mindset: While completing the following drills, picture yourself as a newly-appointed ranking mentor of an ancient order, training students on a remote ice world that is covered in snow and dotted with caves filled with exotic crystals. This particular location was chosen so that you and your students can explore your powers and skills without putting others in danger. Help train your partner, as if you were a patient master, but give them a small push to excel.

Execution:

Begin in the **Attentive Stance**, facing each other as if about to engage in an official spar or duel. Bow to your drill partner, and salute them with your signature flourish. Activate your saber and transition into the **Ready Stance**.

1. Partner A will initiate the first drill, attempting to land a strike with the **Bounty Hunter** technique on Partner B.

Partner B will attempt to prevent the strike with a parry and riposte, using the **Knock Down**.

2. Partner A attacks with the **Maul**, and Partner B defends with the **Separatist Slip**.

3. Partner A attacks with the **Quick Draw** and Partner B defends with the **Big Deal**.

4. Partner A attacks with the **Do or Do Not** and Partner B defends with the **Imperial March**.

5. Partner A attacks with the **Force Push** and Partner B defends with the **Carbon Freeze**.

6. Partner A attacks with the **Torpedo** and Partner B defends with the **Trench Run**.

7. Partner A attacks with the **Spice Run** and Partner B defends with the **Death Sticks**.

8. Partner A attacks with the **Blaster Fire** and Partner B defends with the **Acid Rain**.

9. Both partners deactivate their sabers and complete the drill with a handshake.

Mastery Code: PXXZFZN

Further Study: This partner drill is comparable to "*Kata Geiko*" paired training in kenjutsu and "*Yskudoku Geiko*" in kendo.

Advanced Techniques

In order to master this lesson, simply make sure that you understand its contents so that you have a good idea of what to expect in the lessons to come.

The final third of the techniques in this manual are classified as "Advanced." If you find yourself progressing so quickly that you are forgetting past lessons, it is strongly recommended that you pause here and practice all previous techniques until you can figuratively "do them in your sleep." By the time you've reached this lesson, you would have ideally participated in at least five to ten spars, duels, or tournaments. Hopefully by now, you also have been true to your daily training routine for some time and have found a number of training, sparring, and dueling partners.

Students of the RSA would have typically reached the rank of "Apprentice" in the Rogue Order before completing this lesson. If you belong to a club or dojo, check with your instructor to see if you are deemed ready to move on in their program before studying these advanced techniques.

Advanced Attacks and Ripostes:

The next lessons you will come across are "Composite Attacks." These are techniques that require the highest level of skill and are comprised of multiple steps with multiple targets. You will find techniques that are more advanced versions of previous ones or are amalgamations of a few maneuvers you already have mastered. Advanced attacks also will require you to step into more volatile situations, relying upon your speed and advanced skill to gain the upper hand, in the spirit of "preemption in a state of mutual confrontation." Remain levelheaded and calm as your opponent aggressively attacks, and meet them with overpowering resolve, overcoming them even at the peak of their attack. Some of these techniques require you to come face-to-face with an opponent, lock blades in the tension of the moment, and still come out the victor. You will learn how to take advantage of even the most subtle weaknesses in your opponent's form.

While advanced ripostes are similar to the intermediate ripostes, the advanced attacks you will learn focus on making the most of every privileged position in which you find yourself. Rather than making a satisfying strike and retreating, you will be encouraged to score multiple points in a row, exploiting the same opening in your opponent's defenses multiple times. Therefore, it falls upon your best judgment when to utilize such aggressive maneuvers. For example, if you are sparring with a fellow student of much lower skill, it may be prudent to only strike once and retreat. Failing to parry even one attack may give them a sufficient challenge to overcome. Failing to parry a rapid-fire sequence of attacks may be so overwhelming to them that they lose hope of ever progressing past their current level of expertise. Always remember that you are not the enemy of your opponents. You are merely their allies in their quest for self-refinement.

At this stage, now more than ever, you will be called upon to get inside the mind of your opponent. If you only see the world through your limited perspective, you are like a prisoner, at the mercy of those without. Instead, expand into your opponent's mind space. Try to see each match through their eyes. If you were trying to defeat yourself, what measures would you take? Your practice and your dedication to your studies by now have hopefully allowed you to strike and act reflexively and without any extra thought. Therefore, your mind should now be freed to leave your own objectives and imagine those of your opponent. Feel their rhythm. They must show you their patterns, so recognize them. Memorize how they take aim, raise their arms, breathe in, and exhale as they swing down for a strike. If their rhythm is bad and they are uncoordinated, you should realize this within the first seconds of the match.

When practicing on advanced techniques, keep an eye on interrupting your opponent's rhythm. Striking with a sword is like attacking someone armed with a bow and arrow. Strike them while they are in their preparatory motions, just like you would strike a bowman as he is pulling back on the bowstring. If you attack at the same time they attack, your match devolves into a mess. However, if you attack slightly before, you have gained the key advantage. It is that small sliver of time that makes all of the difference. When an opponent is your equal and performing at their best, smother their moment to shine before it comes. This is the relentless mindset of an advanced duelist, and calls to the Japanese tradition of "Killing the spirit," or "*Ki wo korsu*,"in which a duelist focuses on gaining the upper hand by breaking the concentration and composure of one's opponent, forcing them to assume the defensive position.

Study these techniques carefully and master them with a high personal standard of excellence. Only then will you have what it takes to become an unstoppable champion.

Mastery Code: 2XA9SRF

Further Study: On techniques like these, feel free to look up the "Three Preemptions," "Stomping a Sword," and "Becoming the Opponent" in the *Fire Scroll* of Musashi's *Book of Five Rings*. In addition, you can look into "*Seme*," "*Renzoku Waza*," "*Tsubazeriai*," and "*Hiki Waza*" in kendo.

Form 1 Advanced High Attack

Summary: Your opponent will only realize their hasty error too late. Although this attack plays like a riposte, you are actually eliciting a response from your opponent as a part of your plan. Point your saber to the ground, inviting an attack to your high target zone. Step forward with your left foot, knock your opponent's response to the left, step to your right, and drop a diagonal cut to their neck. Movements in this lesson are similar to those found in the Floor Escape, Royal Rap, Maul, and the Bounty Hunter.

Execution:

1. Assume the Ready Stance.

2. From the Ready Stance, slowly drop the tip of your saber down so that it points to the ground in front of your right toes. (No twist of the wrist is needed.) Keep your arms relaxed and mostly extended. Bend your knees to lower your body a few inches and roll your hilt only a few degrees clockwise.

3. (If you are feeling exceptionally brave, you may even touch one knee down, or stand holding your saber casually with just one hand, pointing it forward.)

4. Once your opponent lifts their saber up in preparation for an attack, breathe in. (In the next step, you will interrupt their swing down (or across) with your blade, already primed to spring diagonally up from the low right.)

5. Take a regular step forward with your left foot and strongly knock their saber to your left. Continue your hands in the upward motion until they are over your head. (This is important to safely avoid injuring your opponent's face in

the following steps). Swivel the tip of your blade overhead to the left and back.

6. Immediately take a massive right step diagonally to the right. As your blade swivels to the right, swing it diagonally down to strike your opponent's neck, just above their inside shoulder.

7. (Bonus Strike: Bounce your blade down, around your opponent's shoulder and target their inside flank if you are able.)

8. Pivot on your left foot to take a large right step back, and then slide your left foot back into the Ready Stance.

Checking Your Form: While your saber is pointing down, it should feel comfortable and be in line with your entire left arm. Although you appear to be at a disadvantage in this position, your body should be ready to spring into action as you keep your core tight and your shoulders down. Before your opponent launches their attack, keep your mind calm and at ease. This will make you appear disinterested and vulnerable. (Such a relaxed demeanor can be infectious.) Maintain this composure even during the attack. Your cool determination may surprise your opponent even more than a fear-filled overreaction. As you swing your saber up, your left hand should push your pommel down and act as an anchor, the center axis of rotation. After catching your opponent's blade, safely keep your saber pointed up to avoid injury to your opponent's face.

Mastery Code: 88H7SW5

Further Study: This technique is comparable to attacks via invitation in kenjutsu, the "Fifth Technique" in the *Water Scroll*, and "Infection" from the *Fire Scroll* of Musashi's *Book of Five Rings*.

Form 1 Advanced Chest Attack

Summary: The time has come to give your rival a taste of your power and unleash a terrible storm, an eruption of fury on your opponent with a swarm of relentless attacks too quick and numerous to parry. If done properly, you will make six strikes, one right after the other, earning six points in a row. Raise your saber high, then swing down diagonally from your left targeting your opponent's outside shoulder, followed by the same to the other shoulder, then target both arms with horizontal slices (similar to the Blaster Fire technique), then move on to upward diagonal slices to each flank. Whether or not you make contact on any of these strikes, continue on to the next target as if you did. Each transition is done with a spin of the hilt over the head.

Execution:

1. Assume the Ready Stance.

2. Slide your right foot forward, slightly to the left of your opponent's blade (from your perspective).

3. Take in a deeper-than-usual breath. Lift your saber vertically, high up so that your hilt is directly over your head with its blade pointing behind you.

4. As you slide your left foot so that your feet are back in the ready position, slice your saber downward in a straight and controlled diagonal line from the left so that the tip of your saber strikes your opponent's outside shoulder. Release a compressed "hiss" of air with each strike, while reserving some air for future strikes.

5. Eye your opponent's blade. As you have an advantage by planning many steps ahead of them with the attacks to come, their blade should fall into the trap of "playing catch-

up," following your saber as you continue on with this sequence. (However, if they anticipate a movement, simply skip the step in this sequence that they are protected against, and score a hit with the next step.)

6. Reverse the motion of your blade, swiveling it back and up over your head and down in a diagonal slice from the right to their inside shoulder.

7. Rebound your saber back up over your head. Yet this time, when the blade points backward, drop your left arm so that the saber emerges from behind your left side.

8. Horizontally strike the side of your opponent's (outside) upper arm from the left, and again reverse the motion to bring your saber up and over your head.

9. Come down on the right side, horizontally striking your opponent's inside arm.

10. Swivel the saber overhead again, this time dropping the saber all the way down to your left hip before slicing diagonally upward from the lower left to the upper right, targeting your opponent's outside flank.

11. Make the final strike on your right side by swiveling your saber and bringing it to your right hip, and cutting diagonally upward from the lower right to hit your opponent's inside flank.

12. Take primed steps backward into the Ready Stance.

Checking Your Form: Maintain a "crushing" and "overpowering" mindset, with an unrelenting aim to completely overwhelm your opponent. For best results, apply psychological pressure by stepping forward with each strike. Preserve your posture (STAND) throughout all parts of this technique. It is to be executed as a quick sequence and in rapid-succession in order to overwhelm your opponent so that they lose track of your movements. Each attempt should be made with dedication, and not as a feint. After landing a successful strike, tighten your grip on your saber to avoid it being knocked too easily to the side. During your practices, follow through with each movement, tracing and retracing a large letter X, with a line across its middle, in the air.

Mastery Code: BP3F4GD

Further Study: This technique is comparable to the "Crushing" technique in the *Fire Scroll*, of Musashi's *Book of Five Rings*, and follows a pattern similar to the *"Happo Giri Kata"* in Iaido, featuring kenjutsu's *"Hidari Joho Giri"* and *"Migi Joho Giri."*

Form 1 Advanced Core Attack

Summary: Based upon the ceremonial "cleaning" maneuver in iaido, in which a blade is whipped to the side in order to flick blood off of it, this technique calls for unyielding fierceness. You will make two ruthless cuts, one right after another, like writing the number 66. Begin with a downward slice to your left, and cut across your opponent's core, horizontally to the right. Bring your saber over your head, back to your left side, and perform the horizontal slice a second time.

Execution:

1. Assume the Ready Stance.

2. Take medium (primed) steps toward your opponent in order to get into proper striking distance while maintaining your guard.

3. Raise the middle point of your hilt to your eyes and breathe in.

4. Slice your saber straight vertically downward, and then to your right in an L shape (as if to strike your opponent's outside flank).

5. Once your blade sinks below your opponent's hands, pull your left hand to the left and your right hand and saber to the right, building tension. Break through your left fingers' grip, releasing the tension. Twist your right hand so that your palm is facing downward, and abruptly cut horizontally across your opponent's stomach. Breathe out.

6. Continue with the motion straight to your right until your right arm is fully extended. (Keep your feet in the home

position and your saber pointing forward and to the ground, not to the right.)

7. Once your right arm is fully extended, twist your wrist to point your saber up and behind you, with your right palm facing upward.

8. Flex your arm and bring your saber over your head and to the left side of your head in an arcing motion. (Your right elbow should be pointing toward your opponent's throat.) Breathe in.

9. Take a wide step to the right with your right foot and immediately slice horizontally a second time across your opponent's core from that position. Breathe out. Stop the motion once your right arm is fully extended, while keeping the tip of your blade pointing forward and downward.

10. Return your left foot back and to the side of your right. Pivot on your right foot to turn your body to face your opponent again in the Ready Stance.

Checking Your Form: Check your V-grip before and after performing this double-strike. If your opponent's core is too well guarded, you may still use this technique to knock their saber aside with the first swing and strike above their hands on the second. When you flick your blade, you need only curl two or so left hand fingers around your hilt to build the tension, and then slip them off to release it. The pressure should not be great enough to misdirect your blade, only to call back to the original purpose of this motion and to set up the performance of the rest of the technique just with your right hand. Since you are not taking many steps, remember to keep your motion conserved and precise, without excess.

Mastery Code: 74W6TVR

Further Study: This technique is comparable to *"Eshin-ryu Chiburi"* and *"Omori-ryu Chiburi"* in iaido and *"Hidari Kesa Giri"* in kenjutsu.

Form 1 Advanced Low Attack

Summary: Only the quicker opponent will claim the high ground. If done correctly, this maneuver will bring you three points as you hit your opponent's inside arm and both legs. If done incorrectly, you leave your upper body open to attack. Therefore, the great risk and reward should be considered and measured. Does your opponent overestimate their own abilities? Bring a swift end to the match from a position of strength. Raise your saber over your head at the same time your opponent does the same. Step to the left and strike down on your opponent's inside arm and continue the motion downward. Bring your hilt near your right hip, then cut to your left to slice across both thighs while making your escape past your opponent. (This technique shares similarities with the Maul.)

Execution:

1. Assume the Ready Stance.

2. Breathe in as you lift your saber straight up (this can be done in response to your opponent assuming the same position before an attack). Keep raising your saber until the hilt is centered over your head and the tip of your blade is pointing behind you.

3. Even before your first hit is made, take a large step to the left with your left foot, widening your stance. (This should be a sufficiently large step to avoid strikes from above.)

4. In the moment just before your opponent can make a move, lower your left hand straight down, slicing downward, but swivel your saber with your right hand so that your blade swings to the right. Target the side of your opponent's inside arm.

5. Continue in the motion, as if it is just one big cut, slicing straight downward. Briefly point your saber's tip to the right as you bring your right foot forward and to the left (in walking step) to pass the side of your opponent.

6. Turn the palm of your right hand upward as it approaches your right hip. Immediately swing your blade upward and to the left, into your opponent's inside leg (just above the knee), leading with the hilt of your blade.

7. As you dash forward and to the left, drag your saber so that it slices across both of your opponent's legs behind you.

8. Once the tip of your blade has passed the second leg, hover your saber in place, center your body around it, and return to the Ready Stance.

Checking Your Form: Between your first downward strike and your second horizontal slice, there should be no pause. Rather, one movement should flow seamlessly into the other. Keep your upper arms tight against your body to add strength and stability to your strikes. Time your leftward step so that it is completed in the same moment that your saber is raised. When cutting low, ensure that you are leading with the hilt of your saber so that your blade can slice across both legs, rather than being stopped by one.

Mastery Code: 3Z7RCG3

Further Study: This lesson is comparable to the "Second Technique" in the *Water Scroll* of Musashi's *Book of Five Rings* and "*Migi Joho Giri*" in kenjutsu.

Form 1 Advanced Outside Arm Attack

Summary: You'll begin this technique on one side of your opponent, then end up on the other. While taking careful steps, like the shifting allegiances of a defecting pilot or trooper, you'll be able to score two points before your opponent can shout "traitor!" Chamber your saber on your right hip, then clash against your opponent's blade with your hilt high and tip low. Step to the left and slice your opponent's outside arm. Step again past your opponent to strike the back of their outside leg. This technique combines movements from the Maul, Death Sticks, Big Deal, Hand Slice, and Smuggler.

Execution:

1. Assume the Ready Stance.

2. Lower your saber and take a large step back with your right foot. Chamber your saber with both hands resting against your right hip. Allow the blade to point back and to your right.

3. As your opponent attempts a downward slice, (or simply remains guarded) step forward with your right foot (into the home position) to close the distance and interrupt their range of motion.

4. Bring your hilt diagonally upward, so that it hovers in front of your left shoulder. Meet your opponent's vertical blade at a perpendicular angle with your horizontal blade. (Your right palm should be close to your face, just below your eyes.) Breathe in.

5. Lift your left hand straight up and point your saber's tip downward. (Your saber should be angled so that their blade

would slide down and to your right if their motion were to continue.)

6. Rather than pushing against your opponent's saber (as they may expect), your blade will immediately bounce down and back away. While keeping your left hand over your head, sweep your saber to your right and behind your head.

7. Bring your left foot diagonally forward and to the left with a walking step. Swivel your saber around the back of your head, to slice right, horizontally into the outside arm of your opponent with the middle third of your blade. Breathe out.

8. Let go of the saber with your left hand. After striking their arm, take a large step with your right foot forward (past their side) and bounce your saber away from your opponent and down to target the back of their outside leg. Breathe in.

9. As your walking step with your right foot touches down, strike the back of your opponent's leg with a one-handed backward and downward swing. Breathe out.

10. Center your body on your saber, face your opponent, and return to the Ready Stance.

Checking Your Form: Keep all steps of the technique in mind from the beginning, so that you step and face your body properly. Do not raise your shoulders while blocking or striking, and keep your knees slightly bent at every stage. After your blades first meet, your left foot's step should be diagonal, and mostly forward, not off to the left side. That step should touch down at the same time your opponent's arm is struck. When striking your opponent's arm, your blade will come down off to the right side of your body. (This is one of the rare cases in which you are not recommended to face your target square on. Rather, you and your opponent should be facing opposite directions as you stand nearly shoulder-to-shoulder.)

Mastery Code: 6WENBTY

Further Study: This technique is comparable to the "*Waki Gamae* stance," "Roof Block," and "Offence by invite" style of techniques in kenjutsu.

Form 1 Advanced Inside Arm Attack

Summary: In certain matches you may feel overwhelmed, as if you have only one last ditch effort left to pull ahead. Against a seemingly more powerful opponent, one must be creative. A strike can be made to your opponent while advancing forward or retreating back. But why not try both? Score a point while stepping in, and one while stepping away after clashing your blades together, as if to send sparks. Raise your saber and strike your opponent's inside wrist while closing the distance between you and your opponent. Once you are face-to-face with tension on your blades, take a retreating step back while striking high up on the same arm. This maneuver is much like an advanced form of the Crystal Mine technique.

Execution:

1. Assume the Ready Stance.

2. Breathe in. Slide your right foot forward (slightly to the right of your opponent's blade from your perspective).

3. Raise your saber's emitter up to eye level and swing down to strike their inside wrist. Breathe out.

4. Immediately "bounce" your saber upward until its tip is pointing above your opponent's head. (This is an important safety measure to avoid eye injury.) Draw your hilt in closer to your core.

5. As if your opponent was pulling you into them via a rope tied around your waist, focus on bringing your hips forward while maintaining good posture. Slide both feet forward until you are both toe-to-toe (using quick and small primed steps).

6. Breathe in. Apply pressure against your sabers, which should be crossing at the closest third of each blade. Ensure that your blade is on the right side, pushing forward and slightly to the left. (The fingers of the right glove of each duelist should be near touching.)

7. Negotiate your saber so that it migrates onto the other side of your opponent's saber. Without warning, push your opponent's saber hard to your right (so that they instinctively draw it to your left).

8. Shift your weight to your right foot and raise your saber slightly in preparation for the strike.

9. While taking a step backward with your left foot, swing your blade diagonally down from the right, hitting the upper inside arm of your opponent. Breathe out.

10. Slice your saber straight back, along with your right foot, and return to the Ready Stance.

Checking Your Form: When stepping forward, push off from your back foot which remains firmly planted. While your sabers are locked together, slowly draw your air in so that the pressure in your stomach helps fuel your arms' strength. Rather than pushing hard with your arms, simply lock them in place and use your legs and core to press forward. Balance yourself equally on both feet until you are ready to strike while retreating. As you do not have time to raise your saber high for the second attack, rely upon the strength of your legs, torso, and hands.

Mastery Code: FVPNESY

Further Study: This technique is comparable to "*Hiki Waza*" (in general), "*Tsubazeriai*," "*Taitari*," and "*Hiki gote*" in kendo. It is also comparable to "The Spark Hit" in the *Water Scroll* of Musashi's *Book of Five Rings*.

Form 1 Advanced Outside Flank Attack

Summary: While similar to the Swarm technique, this calls for a more subtle approach and peaceful mindset. When striking an opponent, you should have a clear target in mind, and also a "Plan B" in case you are parried or your opponent moves away. In this lesson, even your contingency plans will have contingency plans. Your overall goal will be to strike your opponent as many times as possible. You will have six targets, transitioning smoothly from one into another like cascading water falling along the side of a rocky cliff. Raise your saber high, then swing down on your opponent's outside shoulder. If thwarted, immediately aim lower to their outside arm, then to their outside flank. Repeat these steps on the inside shoulder, arm, and flank.

Execution:

1. Assume the Ready Stance.

2. Slide your right foot forward, slightly to the left of your opponent's blade (from your perspective).

3. Take in a deeper-than-usual breath. Lift your saber vertically, high up so that your hilt is directly over your head with its blade pointing behind you. (You'll want to give your saber plenty of altitude and potential energy).

4. As you slide your left foot so that your feet are back in the ready position, slice your saber downward in a straight and controlled vertical line so that the tip of your saber strikes your target. While your left hand drops straight down, your right hand will control the small movements of the blade so that it taps in and away from the body. Release a compressed "hiss" of air with each attempt, while reserving some air for further attempts. Immediately (without

drawing your saber back or adjusting your footing) "bounce" your blade (hovering just over the skin) to the next target, as if it was all done with one clean slice. Follow this targeting sequence:

    a. Outside shoulder

    b. Outside arm

    c. Outside flank

5. Step back into ready position and repeat the above steps again, yet on the reverse side, in a mirrored targeting sequence:

    a. Inside shoulder

    b. Inside arm

    c. Inside flank

6. Slide your left foot backward with a large step and follow it with your right into home position. Return to the Ready Stance.

Checking Your Form: While transitioning between targets, allow gravity to help, and make your movements as small and tight against your opponent's body as possible. Preserve your posture (remember STAND) throughout all parts of this technique. Each attempt should be made with dedication and not as a feint. If you strike true with the first or second attempt, continue on with this sequence in order to score more points. If you are parried or fail to make a strike, simply continue on to the next target without hesitation. With each strike, tighten your grip on your saber to avoid it being knocked too easily to the side.

Mastery Code: WTBPNLS

Further Study: This technique is comparable to "The Chance Hit" in the *Water Scroll* of Musashi's *Book of Five Rings*. It is also done in the spirit of "*Renzoku Waza*" in kendo.

Form 1 Advanced Inside Flank Attack

Summary: This attack is 90% psychological and uses similar movements to those found in the Bounty Hunter, Trench Run, and Hut Slap. Because you are becoming a skilled duelist, you know that you must always keep your end goals in mind but adjust your plans as necessary. In this technique, you will establish a predictable pattern. Chamber your saber in various ways and shift your footing, stance, and saber position, all in order to prompt your opponent to expose their outside shoulder and inside flank. Once your opponent has fallen for the bait, like a weak-minded fool, you'll strike with a diagonal slice to your opponent's neck, just above the outside shoulder, then lean back as you wave your saber in front of you (like the subtle wave of the hand to the right) and strike their inside flank.

Execution:

1. Assume the Ready Stance.

2. Appear confused, uncertain, or conflicted with your body language. Most importantly, establish a predictable pattern of:

    a. Pause
    b. Reposition
    c. Step and Feint

3. Follow this pattern a number of times until your opponent is able to anticipate your movements. When paused, get a feel for your opponent's guards and reflexes. Do they favor one side over the other? Are they quick to riposte low rather than high? What do they do if you fake a powerful attack? Keep all these things in mind. When repositioning, chamber your saber to different sides, onto your hips, and over your

head. Keep your saber moving as if setting up for many different attacks, only to change your mind and reposition again. When you feint, quit the motion early on and pull back. This will make you harmless in your opponent's mind. Experiment with different combinations and false angles of attacks, following your pattern.

4. As soon your opponent's outside shoulder and inside flank are unprotected, and they have come to expect half-hearted feints from you, chamber your saber back into your left shoulder.

5. Spring forward with surprising resolve. (Do not step forward. Rather, shift your weight onto your right foot.) Press your saber up and forward, and strike your opponent's neck in a downward diagonal slice, just above the outside shoulder.

6. Immediately swing the tip of your saber upward and back (in front of your face). Lean back onto your left foot as you take a wide step to the right with your right foot.

7. As your right foot touches down, whip your saber around to strike your opponent's inside flank.

8. Allow your left foot to follow your right into the Ready Stance.

Checking Your Form: Before making your strikes, do not allow your saber to stay in any fixed position. Keep it moving and fluid. In the transition of your saber from the first target to the second (in the "waving" motion), keep your left hand near stationary in front of you, only sinking or raising it slightly. You should rely much more heavily on your right hand to direct and stir the saber around.

Mastery Code: 2UJZ5CD

Further Study: This technique is comparable to "*Tobikomi waza*" in kendo and "On the Teaching of Having a Position without a Position" in the *Water Scroll* as well as "Moving Shadows" in the *Fire Scroll* of Musashi's *Book of Five Rings*. It also comparable to the "*Hidari Kesa Giri*" and "*Migi Ichimonji Giri*" techniques in kenjutsu.

Form 1 Advanced Attack Pattern Drill

Summary: Mastering all advanced attacks is no small feat. If you are equal to the task ahead, then do not slow down or let yourself be distracted from completing this lesson. A partner is not needed for this drill. Instead, you are to picture in your mind this scenario: You have become a capable mentor to others and have discovered an ancient secret lying deep in the ruins of a city forgotten by history. After traveling to the arcane planet and pouring over hieroglyphs, you are met with an armored assassin. As you battle with the assassin, you soon realize that it is not a true opponent, but a dark apparition, a memory of a curse protecting the relics you seek. Nevertheless, it wields a saber and has the power to defeat you if you give it the chance. When you can perform each technique crisply, with perfect form, and with smooth transitions in regular dueling speed and without pause, then you may consider this lesson mastered.

Execution:

1. Begin in the **Attentive Stance**, facing 12:00, and standing in the center point of your practice space. Bow to your would-be assassin (standing at 12:00), activate your saber, and salute with your signature flourish.

2. Transition into the **Ready Stance** and read your opponent closely. Picture their large stature, hidden face, heavy armor, and crackling saber.

3. Drop your saber, pointing it low to the ground a few inches beyond your right foot. Breathe deeply, and wait a brief beat for the assassin to take the invitation to attack first.

4. Your nemesis takes a massive step forward and swings a saber downward to strike your head. While performing the

It's a Trap, knock his saber to the left, and strike down on his neck.

5. Yet when making contact with his neck, your saber passes right through him, as if you were only cutting through mist. Bend your knees and bring your saber's hilt down to your left hip as the mysterious figure, only slightly weakened, escapes to 6:00. Follow your foe with your eyes and turn your body to face him.

6. Before your foe can attack, take an aggressive step (toward 6:00) with your left foot and use the **Swarm** to weaken it further. With each strike, take a walking step forward, forcing the being to walk backward as it narrowly misses the tip of your blade. (Follow through with each strike, practicing the full range of motion.) Step down on your right foot as you make the 6th cut, diagonal up and to the left.

7. The dark assassin then stands its ground and vanishes with a haunting laugh. He reappears directly behind you, red eyes gleaming, with a horizontal slice to your flank. Raise your saber over your head and pivot on both feet to face him (toward 12:00).

8. Step forward with your right foot (returning to home position) and deflect his attack with the first downward slice of the **Order 66** and proceed to slice him twice across his core. You can now see pieces of his shadowy armor disintegrating off of him with each of your strikes.

9. The phantasm vanishes again, reappearing in a full charge toward you at 12:00. You run to face him (returning to the starting center point) and immediately perform the **High Ground** as he attempts to strike from above. As he takes steps forward and to the left, circle around your opponent in order to also drag your saber along the armor in the back of his legs. Yet as you circle back to the center point while

facing 9:00, the ghostly opponent vanishes again with a cloud of smoke.

10. Take two walking steps toward him and perform the **Defector**, finishing by striking the back of the figure's leg behind you and to the right. Turn to face him immediately after (facing the center point and 3:00). As you do so, he wearily turns to face you. Half of his dark armor has visibly dissolved.

11. He attempts to lunge toward you with a vertical slice down, but you interrupt him with the **Spark of Resistance**, striking him on the outside wrist, then on the outside upper arm.

12. He steps back and you pursue him with two walking steps and perform the **Waterfall**. Your first and second attempts to strike his armor fail, on both sides, but you are able to slice into his smoke-like form with each strike to the flank. With the second horizontal slice into the flank, follow your blade as you pivot on your feet to face 12:00 again.

13. You sense that there is no mind to this creature. Therefore, there is no consciousness to confuse or fool. Immediately perform the conclusive strike of the **Mind Trick** (to the outside neck and inside flank) as he attempts a final attack.

14. At last, as your final strike to his flank is made, you hold your position as he completely disintegrates before you, like a heavy mist, scattered by the wind. A frustrated cry erupts from the spectral figure, followed by silence. A deactivated red saber drops to the ground before you.

15. Deactivate your saber. Spin it down and back to your left hip, held in place by your left hand. Face 12:00 in the Attentive Stance.

16. Bow to the disturbed ancient ruins, in gratitude for the epic fight.

Mastery Code: KN4FC2F

Further Study: This drill is comparable to *"Hitori Geiko"* and solo *kata* sequences in kendo, Kenjutsu, and iaido.

Form 1 Advanced High Riposte

Summary: Will you choose the light side or the dark? The honorable warrior will pause when his blade is against his foe's neck, giving them an option to surrender. With this technique you will smoothly transition from a block against a swing to your high target zone, to a dominating diagonal slice to your opponent's neck, showing restraint as it rests against their skin (if only to take a moment to gloat).

Execution:

As your opponent swings their saber downward (or from your left) in an attempt to strike your high target zone...

1. Point your saber to your left and raise both hands above your head, holding your saber horizontal. Breathe in.

2. Angle your saber so that its point drops down slightly and to your left. (When your opponent's saber hits, it should slide down and off to the side.) Push off your back left foot and step diagonally forward and to the right with your right foot.

3. Using primed step, bring your back foot into position behind and to the left of your right. Pivot on your right foot so that you face your target square on.

4. Once your opponent's blade strikes against yours, immediately bounce your saber down and behind you, swiveling its hilt over your head while keeping your arms high.

5. Once your blade is pointing directly behind you, lock your left foot in place and take a large step with your right foot

toward your opponent, bringing you within striking distance.

6. Breathe out as you slice down in a well-controlled and careful strike to your opponent's neck, just above their inside shoulder.

7. Take a large right step straight back, followed by your left, into the Ready Stance.

Checking Your Form: During the initial "block" above your head, you should attempt to reach up to meet your opponent's blade, rather than wait for it. You will thus be redirecting their saber and using their own downward motion against them. This is especially true if you point your blade's tip almost directly down. As with any strike in this manual, you should only exert as much force as necessary to make contact and score a point. If you were attempting to decapitate a deadly foe, you would obviously use more force and speed. Your primed step footwork is key in this maneuver. Remember to practice it often so that it can be performed quickly and naturally. You certainly don't want to fall into the mistake of forgetting your footwork during your drills.

Mastery Code: 3ESWD6E

Further Study: This technique is comparable to the "Roof Block" and "*Migi Kesa Giri*" of kenjutsu.

Form 1 Advanced Chest Riposte

Summary: An aggressive flurry of attacks from your opponent can be overwhelming. When on the defensive, it is one's natural instinct to retreat and back away from the threat. However, running away can make you more vulnerable and even awaken a hunting instinct in your opponent. Sometimes the right way to defend yourself is to close the distance and get in the face of your attacker. This can tremendously diminish their power to attack. You've seen what an aggressive toe-to-toe maneuver looks like with the Spark of Resistance technique. In this one, you'll close the distance and "swamp" your opponent as a defensive move in order to limit their ability to strike you in any way.

Execution:

As your opponent unleashes a flurry of attacks and you find yourself unable to keep up with them...

1. Breathe in, taking in more air than usual. Remain calm and focused.

2. Keep your blade vertical (or at least pointed above your opponent's head) as you take primed steps toward your opponent. Focus on bringing your hips forward first, allowing the rest of your body to follow. Your goal is to come face-to-face, as if you were both comparing height.

3. As you grow closer, limiting the range of motion of the lower portion of their blade, your opponent will soon be unable to reach you with the end of their saber. Apply pressure against your sabers, which should be crossing at the closest third of each blade. Ensure that your blade is above the other, on the right side, pushing forward and slightly to the

left. (The fingers of the right glove of each duelist should be near touching.)

4. Breathe out in pressurized hisses as you keep your arms flexed.

5. Take a miniscule step with your right foot to the side of your opponent's foot, then push off both feet to lean into your opponent as your blade slides up theirs, causing their own saber's tip to point closer to them.

6. Continue to apply pressure and slide your saber up or down in order to cause your opponent to strike themselves with their own saber.

7. Take a large step back with your left foot and bring in your right into the Ready Stance.

Checking Your Form: Only if you keep your blade aggressively "glued" to your opponent's can you limit their range of motion. Be sure to practice this as much as possible with a training partner, so that you get a feel for what it takes to gain control over another's blade with such a technique. A surprising amount of strength can come from controlled breathing. Even a smaller and weaker duelist can perform this technique against a stronger foe if these steps are followed. When toe-to-toe with your opponent, don't just bring your head and legs in close, but ensure your whole body is pushing forward as one.

Mastery Code: LMZYGW8

Further Study: This technique is comparable to the "Comparing Height" and "The Sticky Body" lessons in the *Water Scroll*, as well as the "Sticking Tight" lesson in the *Fire Scroll* of Musashi's *Book of Five Rings*.

Form 1 Advanced Core Riposte

Summary: Has your opponent's telegraphed attacks failed them for the last time? Do you find your opponent's lack of skill disturbing? Teach them a memorable lesson with this aggressive riposte. Although this "choking" riposte comes nearest to threatening the throat of your opponent (compared to all other techniques in this manual), you will actually target and strike your opponent's upper chest. Step to the side, follow your opponent's blade and knock it down. Swing your left side forward to cut with the middle third of the blade to catch your opponent square in the upper chest. Continue to step past your opponent to complete the movement.

Execution:

As your opponent attempts a downward slice or a strike below your hands...

1. Breathe in. Step diagonally forward, but mostly to the right with your right foot. (This will get you out of harm's way.)

2. Now is your chance to take advantage of your opponent's saber being far from their body as they continue with their swing. In the blink of an eye, send your saber downward to knock their blade further down. Aim to cross both blades at their balance at their middle thirds.

3. Take a wide step forward with your left foot, swinging your entire left side close to your opponent. Bring your saber to shoulder level, pointing horizontally to the left.

4. The forward motion from your step should allow you to broadly and easily meet your opponent's chest with the middle third of your blade. Breathe out.

5. Continue past your opponent's side by taking walking steps, starting with your right foot, until you are outside striking distance. In order to avoid uncomfortably crossing your hands, release your hilt with your left hand. Allow your saber to "drag" across your opponent's chest behind you as you take another step.

6. Pivot on both feet to turn your body and face your opponent in the Ready Stance.

Checking Your Form: This movement includes two wide steps. Be sure to bend your knees and don't overextend yourself, or else your lack of recovery will leave you at your opponent's mercy. Did you miss hitting down your opponent's blade? You can still complete the rest of the technique. Hitting the blade down is not necessary, but buys you more time with which to work. While practicing, always attempt to knock the blade straight downward, meeting the middle of both blades. Immediately after, twist your hilt so that your right palm faces directly downward. Aim your right fist at your opponent's inside shoulder (as if to punch them) and twist your saber's hilt with your left hand to bring the blade horizontal.

Mastery Code: XVZBGW9

Further Study: This technique is comparable to the "*Uchiotoshi Waza*" in kendo and "Throat-line *Joho Giri*" in kenjutsu.

Form 1 Advanced Low Riposte

Summary: You may think the greatest duelists are those who are young, with dramatic shows of bravery and risky escapes. However, a true master's skill enhances with age. In this lesson you'll exercise your ability to see deep into your opponent and discover their critical weakness, or "shatter point." This is, possibly, the most difficult riposte in this manual. However, it requires the least movement. How is that possible? Great aim and fortitude is key. After your opponent has raised their hands up before an attack, take a small step forward and press the tip of your blade against their hand, foiling their attempts to swing in any useful direction. As a bonus to your impressive feat, you'll simultaneously score a point.

Execution:

As your opponent raises their saber in preparation for an attack...

1. Assume the Ready Stance.

2. Breathe in. Picture exactly where your opponent's hands are now, and where they must drop in order for them to complete an attack. Target the middle point between those two ends in their range of motion.

3. If necessary, and with small (primed) steps, bring yourself close enough so that you can barely reach your target point.

4. With minimal hand movement, quickly point the tip of your saber so that it lodges itself inside the palm of your opponent's left (lower) hand as they swing downward.

5. Stay in the Ready Stance.

Checking Your Form: When receiving pressure from your opponent's downward swing, ensure that your weight is equally distributed between your feet. Keep your core tight and flex your arms so that you can handle extra weight with ease. Before its use in a duel, this technique requires more practice than usual with a partner. Practice slowly at first to aid in your ability to aim and predict an opponent's movements.

Mastery Code: 5CE2N9A

Further Study: This technique is comparable to *"Osae Waza"* in kendo.

Form 1 Advanced Outside Arm Riposte

Summary: Are you the best fighter pilot in the galaxy? In this technique (similar to the Carbon Freeze), you'll utilize the cool and casual "sliding up" method of redirecting your opponent's blade as seen in the Pilot. Yet this time, you'll step to the left, spin your saber around, and attack down on their outside shoulder, like a fighter pilot working hand and foot controls in order to shoot down a rival.

Execution:

As your opponent swings their saber horizontally or downward, targeting your right arm or wrists...

1. Point the tip of your saber toward your opponent's hands. While keeping the tip in place, pull your hilt over to the right so that your blade will get hit, not your arm or flank. Patiently await your opponent's blade to hit against yours.

2. When contact is made, slide the right side of your blade up the left side of your opponent's blade.

3. As soon as you reach their blade's tip, flick their saber away in a "snapping" motion, off to your right.

4. Breathe in, lift your hands up only slightly, and step to the left with your left foot. While keeping your arms extended in front of you, swivel your saber so that your blade leans from your right, back near your face, and finally to your left.

5. Once your right foot sweeps over to its place in home position, stomp it down, and swing your saber down vertically onto the outside shoulder of your opponent with the last third of your blade. Breathe out.

6. Take a large step back with the left foot and return to the Ready Stance.

Checking Your Form: A common mistake among students is to aggressively meet an opponent's blade and knock it aside as a kind of explosive action. Careful timing and plenty of practice is required before this technique can be implemented. It requires a calm and less panicked approach. As your blade slides up the other, moderately twist your hilt counter-clockwise so that your right thumb is parallel with the floor. This will help prevent your saber being manipulated back. If you begin to lose pressure against your opponent's blade, taking a small forward step with your right foot will help.

Mastery Code: 5PD5MAX

Further Study: This technique is comparable to "*Kote Suriage Men*" and "*Fumikomi* footwork" in kendo.

Form 1 Advanced Inside Arm Riposte

Summary: Almost every technique in this manual involves key footwork, but can you perform an effective riposte while standing your ground? Start this technique while you and your opponent are face-to-face, locking blades. They came in, but do they have a plan for getting out? As they pull back to strike your arm or side, knock their saber down and return the favor. This maneuver is a hybrid riposte combing the Knock Down and the Crystal Mine. It will get you out of a tight spot, but it will take a great deal of skill and timing.

Execution:

As you and your opponent's blades are locked and you stand face-to-face, wait patiently. As your opponent pulls back and targets one of your arms or flanks...

1. Breathe in, and remain utterly relaxed. Eye your opponent's movements, where their blade is pointing, and their footwork.

2. As soon as their blade moves to a side, mirror your opponent's motions, sweeping your saber to the same side to protect your arm and flank.

3. At the soonest opportunity, follow your opponent's blade down with great speed to knock it downward. (This will rebound your saber upward).

4. Continue in the upward motion by horizontally slicing into your opponent's outside arm as they retreat.

5. Breathe out and remain in the Ready Position.

Checking Your Form: When rebounding upward after knocking your opponent's blade down, twist your saber as if you were aiming a cutting edge of your blade toward your target. Imagine cutting "down, then in" as if making a check-mark shape. While practicing, invite a drill partner to randomly alternate the flank on which they attempt to strike you. This will help hone your skills at interpreting an opponent's preparatory actions. When without a drill partner, imagine your opponent's arm to be just barely in reach of the tip of your saber. What if your opponent does not lower their saber to one side? Simply perform the Crystal Mine technique instead to the flank of your choice.

Mastery Code: ML55E24

Further Study: This technique is comparable to the *"Hiki-dou"* and the *"Dou-Uchiotoshi-Kote"* maneuvers in kendo and "The Flowing Water Strike" in the *Water Scroll* of Musashi's *Book of Five Rings*.

Form 1 Advanced Outside Flank Riposte

Summary: Only the greatest of duelists will think more than two or three steps ahead. This gives you an immediate advantage with this technique. Like underground freedom fighters, you'll use unpredictable tactics in order to strike at a key target. Begin with knocking your opponent's blade off to your right, as if to riposte immediately after. Surprise your opponent by again returning to their blade and knocking it upward. This will leave the underside of your opponent's hands and wrists exposed. Step forward and slice horizontally across their forearms from below. Whack, blast, and slash! This technique contains movements similar to those in the All Too Easy, Knock Down, and the Torpedo.

Execution:

As your opponent's blade swings downward to threaten your right side...

1. Twist your body slightly to the right and powerfully sweep your vertical blade to the right in order to knock your opponent's off to the side.

2. Breathe in. Immediately hover your right fist in place while pushing forward with your left hand and up, scooping the tip of your saber to your right, back, and down (past your outside shoulder).

3. When your hilt is above your blade, step forward with your right foot and bring your blade horizontal. (Keep your weight on your right foot) Extend your arms forward and upward in an explosive move to aggressively knock your opponent's saber upward from below. Breathe out.

4. (This will knock your blade slightly downward.) Take aim at the underside of your opponent's forearms. Twist your saber so that its tip swings inward, striking your opponent's arm.

5. Take a large step to the left with your left foot, dragging your blade across both of your opponent's arms from below.

6. Return to the Ready Position.

Checking Your Form: Before your opponent attacks, appear relaxed with a neutral face and serious eyes. Your goal in this technique is to surprise your opponent three times in a row. The first and second deflections of their blade will upset their train of thought. Capitalize on this with the resolute third strike. The key to powerfully knocking your opponent's blade to the side or upward is to use your whole body in the parry. Maintain pressure by flexing your stomach and hissing out small portions of air as needed. Utilize your large leg muscles to move your body at higher speeds. Aim past the current position of your opponent's blade so that you don't merely meet it, you force it away. Do not tense your shoulders or flex your hands too tightly, as that may hinder your ability to move swiftly. After hitting your opponent's saber upward, they may do much of your work for you by raising their saber even higher in order to strike again. Keep a controlled mind and eye on the target, striking like a snake when it is exposed.

Mastery Code: 6ST9B5T

Further Study: This technique is comparable to the "Roof Block" of kenjutsu and the "First Technique" in the *Water Scroll*, as well as "Upset" from the *Fire Scroll* of Musashi's *Book of Five Rings*.

Form 1 Advanced Inside Flank Riposte

Summary: With similarities to Shatter Point, this final riposte requires quick thinking, high levels of skill, and a great deal of practice. You must get inside the mind of your opponent in order to fully anticipate their movements. It is only then that you will appear to have such quick reflexes. In the same moment that they raise their saber in anticipation for an attack, follow their hands up with your blade, and stop their downswing by pressing against the underside of their wrists with your diagonal blade.

Execution:

As your opponent raises their saber and inhales...

1. Point your saber horizontally to the left. Bring it near to your left hip and step (uncomfortably close) toward your opponent with your left foot.

2. Follow your opponent's saber up (raising your hilt diagonally upward toward your right shoulder), and "hook" your saber under their bottom (left) wrist, just behind your opponent's hilt.

3. Exit to the right using walking steps as needed. "Drag" your saber behind you, slicing along the underside of their forearms.

4. Turn to your left and face your opponent in the Ready Stance.

Checking Your Form: This technique must be done instantly, without thinking or preparation. It interrupts your opponent's inhale, and is an "off beat" riposte, striking on the "timing of one." Basically, your stance in the home position, mindset, and V-grip must all be perfect, and ready to make this riposte even before the occasion arises. This is achieved through hours of practice. Keep your wrists in line with your arms as much as possible. When "hooking" under your opponent's wrist, your blade should create a "shelf" that your opponent's hands rest on, making it difficult for them to make any attack. After catching your opponent's downward motion (or, rather, preventing it) drop the tip of your saber downward so that your opponent is prompted to slide their saber down and away from you while you make your escape.

Mastery Code: 7K74GFA

Further Study: This technique is comparable to *"Debana Waza"* in kendo, a "Wrist Counter" in kenjutsu, and the "Fourth Technique" in the *Water Scroll* of Musashi's *Book of Five Rings*.

Form 1 Advanced Partner Drills

Summary: As with the basic or intermediate partner drills, you will need a partner of equal or higher skill, and lots of space, to test your knowledge of all the advanced attacks and ripostes in this sequence. Decide who will be "Partner A" and who will be "Partner B" before starting. Practice each movement slowly at first, alternating who will attack and who will defend, as many times as needed. The attacking partner should attempt to land one or more successful strikes, each and every time. At this level, the defending partner should also always attempt a successful riposte (landing a successful counter-strike). After you have both successfully demonstrated a particular riposte five times against each other, move on to the next drill, until you've mastered all drills in this lesson.

Mindset: While completing the following drills, imagine that you are a member of a council of masters, investigating rumors of a self-exiled member of your order causing trouble. You followed the clues across the galaxy leading you to a planet covered in a towering metropolis with skyscrapers, factories, shopping districts, and a criminal underworld. In the dark alleys below, you finally come face-to-face with the hostile exile. Be ready to defend against harsh attacks from your partner, but don't forget your ultimate goal—to win them over and convince them to return with you to the council, as a friend.

Execution:

Begin in the **Attentive Stance**, facing each other as if about to engage in an official spar or duel. Bow to your drill partner, and salute them with your signature flourish. Activate your saber and transition into the **Ready Stance**.

1. Partner A will initiate the first drill, attempting to land a strike to the neck with the conclusive step of **It's a Trap** on Partner B. Partner B will attempt to prevent the strike with a parry and riposte, using the **No Mercy**.

2. Partner A attacks with the **Swarm**, and Partner B defends with the **Swamp**.

3. Partner A attacks with the **Order 66** and Partner B defends with the **Force Choke**.

4. Partner A attacks with the **High Ground** and Partner B defends with the **Shatter Point**.

5. Partner A attacks with the first steps of the **Defector** and Partner B defends their outside arm by catching Partner A's blade and sliding up it with the **Starfighter**.

6. Partner A attacks with the **Spark of Resistance**, successfully hitting the wrist and closing in, coming toe-to-toe with Partner B, who counter attacks with the **Some Rescue**.

7. Partner A attacks with the **Waterfall** and Partner B defends with the **Upward Insurgence**.

8. Partner A attacks with final strikes of the **Mind Trick** (first targeting the neck) and Partner B defends with the **Foresight**.

9. Both partners deactivate their sabers and complete the drill with a handshake.

Mastery Code: GN6ZZ9V

Further Study: This partner drill is comparable to "*Kata Geiko*" paired training in kenjutsu and "*Yskudoku Geiko*" in kendo.

If you have mastered all 66 lessons before this point, then you have grown powerful indeed. Celebration is in order, for you have mastered all of the Rogue Saber Academy's standard Form 1 attacks, parries, ripostes, and drills!

However, Japanese and East Asian swordsmanship can inspire far more than some 48 techniques and a few practice drills. Furthermore, not all of the amazing kendo, kenjutsu, and iaido techniques learned and mastered by the RSA's instructors could fit into the organized training regimen of the basic, intermediate, and advanced techniques in this manual.

Therefore, more techniques like those you have mastered are available on the RSA's website and may even appear in future publications. Of course, that is without even considering future forms that may be taught by the RSA, including those based upon Western Olympic Fencing, Historical European Martial Arts (or HEMA), and more! To master this lesson, explore the RSA's website to see what bonus lessons and other forms await you there.

Mastery Code: BW2XTNG

MEDITATION LESSONS

WHY DO STUDENTS OF SWORDSMANSHIP so often include meditative exercises in their training? In this chapter, you will find the answer to this question along with instructions on how to engage in three common meditations.

Why Masters Meditate

Increased Focus: Learning saber thrusts, parries, and other techniques is essential to the mastery of the weapon. No less critical, however, is the training of your mind. Almost anyone can swing a sword, yet that is often not what determines victory or loss. Fencing is perhaps the most cerebral of all sports. The champion, in a fraction of a second, must be aware of the most subtle movements and the smallest details that will reveal how and when their opponent will move. Therefore, meditation is employed to increase personal focus. Yet before you can fine-tune your sensing of your opponent, you must first conquer the noisy distractions within your own mind.

Limited Distractions: What is the link between meditative states of consciousness and sword fighting? A duel requires one to have the utmost focus, seriousness, and calm in order to make quick decisions under stress. The invasive and distracting emotions of panic, surprise, doubt, uncertainty, and indifference are natural. They can plague the mind of a duelist, jeopardizing their efficacy. Meditation is a powerful tool in sharpening the mind and avoiding such distraction, especially in the exciting moments of a spar, duel, or tournament.

Health Benefits: Modern meditation techniques have been impressing scientists for decades. Although most of these practices came from ancient religions, there is a growing wealth of empirical evidence showing profound mental, physiological, and emotional benefits that come from daily meditation. If you find yourself skeptical of what meditation can actually offer you, please take a moment to do some research on the subject.

Complete Your Training: For our purposes, the following three specific meditations have been inspired by and developed from traditional techniques and then refined. Each meditation corresponds to a stage of your training. There are three meditations for each form, one for the Basic, Intermediate, and Advanced levels of the art. To truly master a form, you must also have tried out its three meditations. This section is dedicated to describing, in detail, how to properly perform each meditation. Please pay careful attention to the instructions below, as dedication to the technique is often the most important part of the meditative process...

Mindfulness Meditations

Form 1 is the way of wisdom. While knowledge is a vital part of wisdom, the wise also seek to live in a state of mindfulness. Mindfulness is the opening up of your mind to the profound and awe-inspiring facts of the universe. Mindfulness is also an awakening to the deeper feelings within yourself, a cosmos no less vast. The masters of mindfulness meditation train their minds to be keenly aware of the present. They are in control of their thoughts.

Our everyday thinking is comparable to that of a monkey, boisterously and frantically climbing and moving about. We are often short-tempered, frustrated, and easily distracted. With 15 to 60 minutes of mindfulness meditation every day, you will find that your thoughts become more tame and your mind becomes healthier. You will notice a reduction in anxiety, improved learning skills, and greater patience with yourself and others. Our training program focuses on three essential parts of mindfulness meditation: "Focus," "Observation," and "Acceptance."

A Note on Positioning:

All first form meditations are done while kneeling. If this position is distractingly uncomfortable for you, even after a few sessions, you may wish to substitute kneeling with sitting cross-legged in all Form 1 meditations.

Basic: Focus Meditation

The goal of this meditation is to quiet your mind and enhance your fundamental meditation skills by concentrating on one simple thing for a prolonged period of time. The Focus Meditation is comparable to the basic starting stance in any martial art. Once this technique is mastered, you may move on to deeper layers of meditation. Try Focus Meditation at least three times before practicing Observation Meditation.

How to Engage in Focus Meditation:

1. Set an alarm for 15 to 60 minutes. Briefly stretch your arms, legs, and core.

2. Prepare a mat or pillow on which to kneel. (Beginners should do their best to ensure that there is no distracting sound or music.)

3. Stand in the **Attentive Stance** behind your pillow or mat.

4. Step your right foot forward in front of your pillow or mat.

5. Slide your left foot back and sink your body down, kneeling on your left knee. (Your right foot remains in front of you and your right knee is bent.)

6. Place your saber to your left side on the floor. Its emitter should be pointing behind you and its pummel should point directly in front of you.

7. Pick up your right foot and slide it behind you, matching your left foot.

8. Rest your body atop your heels with the top of your toes against the floor and feet overlapping.

9. Keep your back straight in natural good posture. (You may wish to adjust your position atop your mat or pillow to maximize your level of comfort.)

10. Close your fingers together and place your right hand (palm-up) in your lap.

11. Rest your left fingers atop your right fingers and touch the tips of your thumbs together, creating a comfortable "basket."

12. Close your eyes.

13. Breathe in a little through your nose, allowing the air to travel to your stomach. (Your stomach will be where all of the important breathing movements take place.)

14. Pause for a brief moment.

15. Breathe out through your mouth. Be mindful of the rhythm of your breathing, the feeling of air sweeping in and the warm release of tension as you breathe out.

16. After your body has set into a natural pattern of breathing, you may choose an object of focus, depending on your needs or intended results. These objects can be sensations, mantras, possessions, or abstract ideas:

    a. **Sensations** – Beginners are encouraged to focus on their breathing, counting each breath and paying attention to all of the feelings and processes involved. A useful tactic is to count each breath up to 10, then backward to one, cycling through the pattern. Other sensations include the feeling of sunshine on your skin, your heartbeat, the smell of a candle, or even a persistent sound such as the wind or music around you.

b. **Mantras** – A "mantra" is a part of a word, full word, or phrase said in your mind over and over again. A useful technique is to whisper or hum the word as you breathe out. Here is a quick list to get you started: "Ohm," "Calm," "Peace," "Force," "Joy," "Focus," or "Balance." If you eventually find yourself just thinking the word rather than saying it, or letting go of the word entirely so that your mind focuses on nothing at all, then you have made good progress.

c. **Possessions** – Think only of a specific static thing such as a plant by your side, the clouds, your saber, or a book. Be sure that the object does not house complex or negative emotions. An example of a poor choice for this exercise would be a picture of an ex-girlfriend.

d. **Abstract Ideas** – Imagine your favorite color, a blank piece of paper, a simple mathematical concept, etc.

17. Once you have chosen one specific object of focus, slowly let your other interrupting ideas fade away from your mind. In this particular meditation, those ideas are like raindrops that tap on your mind, but soon roll off. The key here is to quiet your mind, and allow only that one object of focus to fill your thoughts. Avoid letting your mind wander, but if it does, do not be hard on yourself. Rather, simply course-correct back to your central object of focus. All other things fade into the background. At first, it will take some time to achieve this level of focus, but with practice, you will be able to attain this deeper level of concentration in less time.

18. Continue to breathe in a regular rhythm and think only of the object of focus until your alarm sounds.

19. Open your eyes and take a few larger breaths.

20. You will stand by moving in a reverse process to how you first knelt. Rise off your heels.

21. Pick up your right foot and step it out in front of you.

22. Pick up your saber with your left hand.

23. Press your left toe into the ground and stand.

24. Bring your right foot back to match your left, returning to the **Attentive Stance**.

25. Stretch and reflect on your experience. Consider how different your body and mind feels. Resume your daily activities.

Further Study: This technique is comparable to *Zazen* (Zen Meditation) and utilizes the *Seiza* position.

Intermediate: Observation Meditation

This meditation is useful for centering your sense of self and grounding your experience of reality within the context of your own body. This sets your thinking into a more organized and logical mode. Observation meditation is a transitional phase, honing your skills for more meaningful experiences to come. You should have tried this type of meditation in six or more different sessions before trying Acceptance Meditation.

How to Engage in Observation Meditation:

1. Follow the instructions for Focus Meditation: Set your alarm, kneel with good posture into position, breathe regularly, and allow all thoughts and distractions to fade away as you concentrate only on the object of focus (such as the sensation of your breathing).

2. Remain in true Focus Meditation for a few moments.

3. When you feel that your mind is properly focused and resistant to distraction, you are in a state like that of being in a tent, sheltered from the noise of the world. Once in this state of mind, mentally open the window of that tent, allowing in just a beam of light from the outside world. With your eyes still closed, you will now afford just a sliver of your attention to receiving the sounds, feelings, thoughts, memories, and other sensations that usually compete for your full attention. You will not, however, dwell on any of these things.

4. Once something bids for your attention (such as the smell of a candle), you may now (rather than instantly letting it fade away) take note of it. In this meditation you will label it with the simplest label possible. For example, the fragrance of the

candle would be labeled "smell." Other labels for things around you may also include, "memory," "sound," "feeling," and so on. Take care not to make judgment calls on these things or become preoccupied with them.

5. Once something has been labeled, you will no longer give it any heed. Let it drift off, to be forgotten, and center your thinking back onto the object of focus.

6. Continue to breathe in a regular rhythm, center your thinking onto the object of focus, and simply label other things that arrive before dismissing them. Remain in this exercise until your alarm sounds.

7. Open your eyes and take a few larger breaths.

8. You will stand by moving in a reverse process to how you first knelt. Rise off your heels.

9. Pick up your right foot and step it out in front of you.

10. Pick up your saber with your left hand.

11. Press your left toe into the ground and stand.

12. Bring your right foot back to match your left, returning to the **Attentive Stance**.

13. Stretch and reflect on your experience. Consider how different your body and mind feels. Resume your daily activities.

Further Study: This technique is comparable to the "*Vipassana*" meditative style.

Advanced: Acceptance Meditation

The modern sciences of psychology and neurology have allowed our society to prod deeply into the workings of the human mind. One of the first insights thus yielded has been the understanding that much of our brain activity is not done consciously. In other words, a large portion of your thinking develops without your attention or direction. We may call this your "subconscious," the active workings of your mind that operate behind-the-scenes. Your subconscious is always working, and can be a vast source of creativity, insight, and breakthroughs. With Acceptance Meditation, and some skill, you will be able to allow the best of your subconscious ideas to rise to the surface.

Now that you have mastered, or at least are comfortable with, Focus Meditation and Observation Meditation, you are ready to increase your skills further and fully embrace the true culmination of these practices. However, simply having tried all Form 1 meditations does not mean you have already discovered all there is to them. Continually revisit them, refining your technique, and you will soon find a vast ocean of benefits awaiting you.

How to Engage in Acceptance Meditation:

1. Follow the instructions for Focus Meditation: Set your alarm, kneel with good posture into position, breathe regularly, and allow all thoughts and distractions to fade away as you concentrate only on the object of focus (such as the sensation of your breathing).

2. Remain in true Focus Meditation for a few moments.

3. Progress into Observation Meditation. Open your mind up slightly, dispassionately labeling the subtle notions that drift your way, and allow them to fade back into obscurity. Remain in this state of mind for a few more moments.

4. At about mid-way through this session, you'll feel it is time yet again for a transition.

5. If you opened a window in your mind's "tent" in Observation Meditation, then you will now perform the mental equivalent of stepping outside your tent. Open your mind completely to the thoughts and prodding of the cosmos. As notions slowly come to your attention, you will give them a simple label, as before, yet you will now also give them a moment to unwrap themselves. It is like you are kneeling by the side of a child who is eager to tell you a story. It is not your job to critique the story being told you. It is not your job to interrupt with judgments or corrections. Rather, you will allow your mind to listen. Let the idea guide you, expressing parts of it you may not have ever before considered. At last, when you feel the idea has yielded the majority of its secrets, you can let it go, like dropping a leaf into a slow moving river. You will then receive the next idea, and the next, freeing yourself of any responsibilities to assess them. This meditation is completely about a controlled and deep listening to the ideas themselves, ideas that may never surface in day-to-day thinking.

6. Continue in this mindset along with your continued regular breathing until your alarm sounds.

7. Open your eyes and take a few larger breaths.

8. You will stand by moving in a reverse process to how you first knelt, returning to the **Attentive Stance**.

9. Stretch and reflect on your experience. Consider how different your body and mind feels. Most importantly, take note of some of the previously unknown understandings you may have gained. It is only at this step that you may critique and analyze them. Resume your daily activities.

Further Study: This technique is comparable to *"Shikantaza"* meditative styles.

WAYS TO CONTINUE YOUR TRAINING

IT CAN BE REMARKABLY SATISFYING after winning a number of spars and duels to look back upon your progress and contemplate how far you have come. Perhaps by now you have increased your collection of sabers, with impressive models from a number of saber-smiths. You no doubt have found that in order to keep your skills sharp, regular practice going over the lessons you have mastered is key. Even some of the greatest and most elderly of kendo masters engage in the same exercises taught to children. We can learn a great deal from their dedication.

In the spirit of *bushido*, and in the tradition of many of the great samurai mentioned in this manual, you no doubt have developed a thirst for even more styles, forms, and techniques to learn. Just as a sword grows dull over time, you know your skills must be ever tested and sharpened. A true master of the sword does not reach a satisfactory skill level, then lock their sword away. Rather, he wanders until he finds greater adversaries, greater challenges, and wiser teachers.

A student of swordsmanship starts off much like a miniature bonsai tree. Did you know that these plants are just common trees? If planted in the forest, they have the potential to grow to spectacular sizes. However, they have been limited, and cultivated in a small pot. With such a small amount of earth, their growth is stunted.

If you limit your study of swordsmanship to one book, one academy, or one program, then you likewise stunt your growth. In this chapter, a short list of options have been assembled in order to inform you of the paths you can take in order to continue your training.

The Rogue Saber Academy

The Rogue Saber Academy is a tuition-free online training school that instructs its students in dueling, meditation, and more. Given the strengths and weaknesses of online instruction compared to in-person training, the RSA has been carefully crafted to serve the greatest number of students with the best from both options.

It is with great pleasure that the governing council of the RSA presents the lessons and resources in this volume. They represent enormous effort, but also a source of pride for all involved.

When contemplating how you would like to continue your education as a swordsman, you'd be wise to look into what the Rogue Saber Academy has to offer. It's the RSA's mission to connect duelists, train knights, and build community. In order to meet these and other ambitions, a number of online resources have been made available for you, and for anyone who shares your passion for this new sport. In this section, you'll get a small idea of what you can find on the RSA's website. If you haven't yet, be sure to give it a look!

Online Resources

The Duel Finder System: Any visitor to the RSA's site who creates an account can use the spectacular Duel Finder System. It includes a network of codes, forms, and maps designed to connect duelists, facilitate an optional point system for wins and losses, and allow duelists to schedule matches and rate each other's sportsmanship after the fact. Simply click on your area of the map, select an icon representing a nearby duelist, and invite them to a spar, duel, or even to a tournament!

Online Training Videos: While some techniques are only found in print, most come in a detailed text version (as seen in the lessons above) and also in a companion video lesson, as a pair. The RSA's training videos provide additional instruction and valuable demonstrations at dueling speed. At least two training videos are uploaded by the RSA each month until all lessons in a particular form are made available. As an added bonus, a video's comment section is a great place to ask the instructor questions.

The Rogue Order of Knights: The RSA hosts a modern order of knights from around the world, and you are welcome to join! Yet the rank of knighthood is one that must be earned. In order to move up the levels and ranks of the Rogue Order, an initiate must agree to follow "The Duelist's Code of Honor," pass certain trials, perform certain acts of service (or "quests") and, of course, master the combat saber.

Saber-Day Celebrations: Did you know there was a holiday commemorating the combat saber? Mark your calendar for the weekends surrounding April 4th! Throw parties, buy new sabers for your collection or as gifts, and participate in massive celebrations and tournaments. Be sure to visit the RSA each year to find out which celebrations are taking place near you!

Community Building: The RSA provides many resources to the saber enthusiast community such as a database of saber-smith reviews, message boards, a private messaging system between students, and the chance to earn badges, patches, Duel Credits, and digital rewards as you help the community grow.

Additional Lessons and Forms: As more students join the academy, bonus lessons describing FORM 1 techniques beyond those covered in this book, companion books to this one, and even techniques from other forms (inspired by completely different schools of swordsmanship) will be made available.

Other Options

It is an exciting time for the students of swordsmanship. Numerous paths are available for anyone who wishes to continue their training. The following list of training program types is by no means comprehensive, but will give you a feel for the terrain. Online, you may find information on at least three or four well-known academies that fit into each of the categories below. Before settling on one, however, be sure to take a moment to consider all of your options:

Formal Kendo, Kenjutsu, or Iaido Classes

These three Japanese schools and disciplines stem from the traditional skills of the samurai. A spiritual respect for the *katana* and other traditional swords is nurtured, and high self-discipline is achieved. In these schools of swordsmanship, the vital code of *bushido* (the honorable way of life of the samurai) is laced within all aspects of the curriculum. Students are expected to show great respect for their *sensei* and engage often in meditation.

In **Kendo** (the most popular of these three schools), you'll be able to duel with peers with a non-lethal sword made of bamboo slats and leather wraps known as the *shinai* and participate in competitions around the world. You will learn how to quickly and efficiently strike the head, gloves, sides, and throat of your opponent. Fortunately, all duelists are protected with extensive armor. While dueling, you will score points by landing a proper strike as long as you also keep the correct posture and the proper spirit. It is a highly respected discipline available to men, women, the elderly, and the young.

Kenjutsu is a much older discipline, and is a direct predecessor to kendo. In kenjutsu, you'll often use a wooden sword, the *bokutō*. In some classes, you will use the steel *katana*, but not against sparring partners. Kenjutsu has an extensive and varied library of styles, attacks, guards, counterstrikes, and specialized techniques. You will often learn routines, or *kata,* in which you follow memorized patterns of attacks and maneuvers.

If you wish to challenge yourself to emulate the sternness, dedication, and deadly precision of the samurai, then you may want to try **Iaido.** Referred to as the martial art of quick-drawing, masters of iaido learn in impressive detail how to draw their sword, whip it through the air, and dispose of imagined enemies using the most traditional of techniques. Before the execution of *kata,* the master of iaido will bow to their steel sword out of respect for what it symbolizes.

These classes usually come at a reasonable price, typically offering years of continued instruction. Of course, you'll need to leave your saber at home, but you will be directly learning the styles of combat that inspired the choreography of the first Star Wars films. Once home, you'll be able to implement what you learn with some modification. If you do not see, in your online searches, a teacher of any of these Japanese disciplines near you, it may help to contact a local martial arts dojo and ask if any of the teachers there know of a master of kendo, kenjutsu, or iaido nearby.

Western Fencing Classes

With its roots in the rise of civilization itself, the modern sport of fencing has evolved into a highly reformed discipline. Western fencing has three forms: Foil, Epee, and Sabre. The equipment and tuition for these classes are not cheap. The good news, however, is that fencing clubs and school programs can be fairly easy to find in many parts of the world. A good place to start looking for a fencing club is your nearest university or college. The swords in these styles are dramatically different from your combat saber, so it would best be left at home. The purchase or rent of a foil, epee, or fencing sabre will be required to participate. Joining this discipline means taking part in a world-renowned and well established sport. Western fencing is filled with the high-class traditions of true gentleman and ladies. Remarkably, it is a sport that has boasted a continued presence in the modern Olympic Games since their inception.

At the time in which this book is written, the Rogue Saber Academy does not offer classes inspired by Western fencing. However, with enough expressed interest, we'd be happy to create the course!

Anachronistic and HEMA Societies

Growing recently in popularity is the study of "Historical European Martial Arts" or "HEMA." These sword fighting techniques are based upon texts from the Middle Ages that have become widely available thanks to modern technology. It has given rise to large troupes of dedicated re-enactors who dress up as medieval knights and choreograph epic jousts and duels with period-accurate weapons. Many of these troupes have even taken these arts a step further to standardize rules in the emergence of a new armored sport. You may even have HEMA tournaments taking place in your community right now!

Reenacting the past can be thrilling, and the wielding of such iconic weapons can be fulfilling (if not at first daunting). Joining such societies for lessons may be free or may come with a small charge, depending on the group. Getting in touch with these societies is mainly a matter of careful internet searching.

Would you like to see an official RSA Form dedicated to HEMA techniques, perhaps with an emphasis on techniques that utilize the cross-guarded combat saber? Be sure to have your voice heard!

Online Videos From Fellow Fans

As we progress down this list of options, we come across training programs in which you can use your combat saber. Increasingly common are dedicated fans of the Galaxy far, far away, eager to share with you their interpretation of the laser-sword techniques shown or described in their favorite stories.

Of course, one downside to going in this direction with your training is that you cannot be sure how effective these new techniques will be. They are commonly created in isolation, with a strong emphasis on style over practical usage. On the other hand, you may be surprised with just how clever these techniques prove to be.

If you are looking for instructions on how to perform fancy spins and flourishes, this source of instruction is particularly valuable. These creative resources can typically be accessed online for free on video sharing sites or on dedicated fan websites. While it may be tempting to dismiss these fan-made forms off hand, the sheer imaginative potential of our community has produced some innovative maneuvers. In all, the most important thing to be gained from these tutorials is lessons from a fresh perspective.

Training Manuals

EBooks and guidebooks, such as this, are great ways to learn a large number of techniques in a short amount of time. In them, you can add your own personal notes and highlight key steps. In the sunny outdoors, physical books offer major advantages over videos and digital media. They can be great time-savers when meeting with others face-to-face. When hosting your own club or when preparing lessons for a dojo filled with students, training manuals are indispensable.

However, when not paired with detailed photos, illustrations, or companion videos, manuals lose a significant amount of teaching power. Another downside to learning from print is that a student tends to be on their own as they progress. Anyone in that boat is welcome to go online and bring the skills learned from a book into spars and duels with the students of the RSA!

The supreme honor and distinction of being the first saber training manual does not go to this volume, but rather to Carey Martell's *"Stunt Lightsaber Combat For Beginners: The Unofficial Guide to Dueling Like a Jedi"* (published in 2015 by Martell Books). Although it wasn't used in the production of this book, students seeking more training are still encouraged to give it a read!

Choreography and Performance Groups

If costumes, crowds, and good causes match your style, then this is an option to consider. It is the most common option for face-to-face training with the combat saber. These groups offer classes in twirling and flourishes, accompanied by staged sparring routines. Sometimes, these services are only geared toward children, designed for maximum safety and immersion in a fan experience. Other times, the group is dedicated only to physically-challenging choreography (based upon intense cinematic or stage choreography) in preparation for stunning performances with rehearsed movements.

These groups often perform at charitable events and are, to a large extent, the face of the saber community. Price of admission and the usefulness of their techniques in a fight will vary. Even if a group such as this does not provide dueling instruction, their stunning displays, dedication, and sheer physical mastery makes them no less worthy of study. If one such group is near you, be sure to join their ranks.

Online Dueling Academies

These schools (such as the RSA) take a massive step up from the online fan videos. They typically focus on sets of more serious techniques that are vigorously tested and optimized for competitive sport. The techniques taught by online academies can be fan-made, based upon historic forms, or some hybrid of both. Instruction is usually provided for free or at a low cost, and instructors tend to be available to answer any questions.

The advantage online academies have over other training options is that they can reach a wide audience, granting students all over the world the chance to learn from their videos, message boards, and other online resources. Students of online academies also have the convenience of studying from home, at their own pace.

One notable downside is that students of these academies often find themselves separated from their classmates by great physical distances. As a result, finding dedicated sparring partners and others to check their mastery during the training process can be difficult. (Should any student of a different academy find themselves in such a situation, they are welcome to utilize the RSA's Duel Finder System in addition to any of the services already at their disposal.)

Local Dueling Academies and Dojos

Prove your skills with the saber! In these physical meet up groups, local training programs, and dedicated facilities, regular classes are taught and spars are fought, just as you would see with dojos teaching Kung fu or Karate. These schools represent the heart of our sport, and have a great deal to offer.

What kind of techniques are taught in these dojos? That is a tricky question to answer. It is often the case that their exact fighting styles qualify as proprietary information, and public access to their specifics is not available. However, your local instructor probably offers free introductory lessons, so don't hesitate to ask for a preview into what their program is like.

Research each local academy to get some understanding of what they offer. Sometimes the club is formed to teach newly-constructed forms to eager students in preparation for grand internal competitions. In other cases, the organization assembles only during special events each year (such as conventions) for truly epic tournaments and training. Other academies have even refined and publicized their system so well that it is taught by multiple masters across a number of different countries.

The great benefit that comes from these programs is that they allow students to interact with instructors in person. An instructor can give suggestions and make corrections to form in real time, and a strong sense of community and unity can come from the student body. If you have the means to create such a local dojo, feel free to use the lessons in this book as a foundation for your own program!

Although these academies are truly awesome, their downside is that they only serve the small amount of combat saber enthusiasts within traveling distance to their events. In addition, many of them are competitive businesses and face local market pressures. If interest declines, they may be forced to move on to teach different martial arts. Finally, they can only grow as quickly as their techniques are taught to successive generations of instructors. Even if you are currently dedicated to a different program or are not able to participate at a local academy or dojo, you can still support it by inviting those around you to give it a try.

If you live in the vicinity of one of these saber dojos or local academies, have trust in their program, have the time to make it to their training classes, and can afford the price of admittance, then what are you waiting for? Be sure to take full advantage of the program if at all possible. Doing so encourages the further development of even more local training programs. Imagine how the sport will grow with at least a dozen local masters in every major city, eager to bring in new students!

School and Community Clubs

There is nothing quite like a dueling club. These organizations are the casual younger brothers of the local academies and dojos mentioned above. They are typically non-profit organizations that offer training, exercise, and service to the local community. Usually, a group of fans and enthusiasts get together weekly, study from a manual or set of videos, spar, hold tournaments, and have an overall great time. If you live in a community with such a club, or live near a college, university, or high school that supports such a club, join it today! It is a great way to expand your skill set, make life-long friends, and have a ton of fun.

If your particular school or community does not have such a club, then why not create one? With the steps and advice you'll find in the next chapter, creating your own saber club has never been easier.

STARTING YOUR OWN SABER CLUB

AFTER LEARNING A FEW DUELING TECHNIQUES, most of us are not content with the occasional spar and duel. We want to pass on what we have learned. A great way to do this is by creating a saber club in your school or community. Here are a few useful tips for starting your own club:

1. **Training Manual**: Assemble a collection of sparring and dueling rules and techniques that can be shared and practiced at weekly meetings. What is that? You are already holding a physical copy of an awesome book with all of those things and more? (You're welcome!)

2. **Saber-smith Recommendations**: Before you gather friends together in a club, make sure you already have your own combat-ready saber. At current prices, it may be prohibitively expensive to attempt to buy a high quality saber for each member (yet you are welcome to give it a try). Instead, it may be wise to make a list for club members of recommended websites to visit in order to purchase their own combat sabers (or saber parts). Do a little research online before making the list. Once it is complete, make copies. Feel free to start your research with the RSA's page of reviews:

   https://www.roguesaber.com/sabersmiths.php

3. **Substitute Saber Recommendations**: After your club members order their combat sabers, it may take a few weeks before they arrive in the mail. In the meantime, you can encourage them to still attend club meetings while bringing a substitute saber of some kind. Would you like your club members to buy toy lightsabers? Would you rather they come from a hardware store with PVC pipes or wooden dowels? Perhaps inviting them to purchase and bring with them a *bokutō* or *shinai* will help them connect more to the historical roots of each movement. Consider which option you like best, but make it very clear that those with combat sabers should not spar or duel with those armed only with substitutes, for safety reasons.

4. **Starting Members**: Rather than attempt to start an entire club on your own, wrangle together a handful of close friends, classmates, or even roommates who have at least a small interest in the sport. This will help you spread the word, share the workload, and encourage a better turnout for your "Interest Meeting." Ask your friends what they would like to do in each meeting, how often they'd like to meet, and so forth. Ideally, this stage of your club formation will take place at least a month before your first planned meeting. In many cases, however, you'll be able to set up a new club in under a week.

5. **Prepare Your Case**: In some schools and communities, almost anyone can start a club for any reason. In others, however, you must convince the school or community leaders that your club meetings will be safe, educational, build character, and benefit the community. If you're asked by officials to "make a case" for your saber club, you can begin your presentation with stating how the study of these historic techniques provides a connection to history and culture. It may help to emphasize that the techniques to be shared, practiced, and used have been carefully optimized with safety in mind, and do not (with a small number of exceptions) require any safety gear. Share what you have learned about *bushido*, and the Rogue Saber Academy's

own Code of Honor, as well as the service projects performed and promoted by the RSA's order of knights. These important parts of the sport can be found on the webpage dedicated to the Rogue Order.

Of course, if your club is expected to teach its members values and engage in community service, remember to make that an actual part of what you do.

6. **Meeting Location**: Speak to your student/community representatives or officials to get an idea of what spaces are available for such a club to meet. (You may need to "make your case" for your new club, even at this early stage.) Officials can typically be found online, in student centers, high school offices, or perhaps at a city's chamber of commerce. Is a certain gym available on Wednesday nights? Is the school's soccer field free on Friday mornings? Is there a stage or dance studio that is not in use? Do some digging until you've found a suitable space. More often than not, a simple field on campus or within a city park will make a great starting location. However, if cold or stormy weather is an issue where you live, you may want to prioritize indoor locations.

7. **Meeting Times**: Talk with your starting members and consider your options for a meeting location. Look at similar school or community sport clubs, hobby clubs, or performing arts clubs to see when they meet, and how often. All these variables should be taken into account when planning meeting times. Do your best to have your club meet at times similar to these other clubs, but not at the same time. This will allow your future members to better attend your club while also belonging to another. As always, don't forget to take regular work or class schedules in mind. "Thursdays at 6:00 PM" or "Saturdays at noon" tend to be the kind of meeting times most people prefer.

8. **Funding**: In most cases, more people will want to join your club if there are no membership fees. If your club does have membership fees, many who love the sport may become disinterested in your club. After all, you'll already be asking many of them to buy new combat sabers which can potentially cost them over $1,000 each. If you must pay fees in order to secure a meeting space and/or satisfy some other charge in relation to being an official club of your school or community, then you may want to consider charging members a small one-time or ongoing membership fee. In the spirit of inclusivity, do your best to keep that fee as low as possible.

9. **Official Authorization**: As soon as you have a handful of starting members (at least five or so) and you have a set time and place for your meetings, seek out those in your school or community who are in charge of authorizing new clubs. Typically, a phone call to a community center, library, student resources office, or to a similar club will help you find out who to call next. Before making any official announcements about your club, be sure to pay any fees and fill out any paperwork necessary in order to be given the green light. Completing this step often leads to your club being added to club lists, directories, and other resources available to the student body or local public.

10. **Initial Promotion**: By now, you probably have an idea of what most clubs do to spread the word about their first meeting. Create colorful and eye-catching posters, flyers, and online posts with brief information and pictures about what your club is, what you plan to do, and when and where your first meeting (your "Interest Meeting") will be. Cast a wide net by inviting the greatest number of people possible. This step may take a lot of your time, as you find out where to best advertise your club, but it will really pay off.

11. **Who is in Charge?** As with any powerful army or successful business, strong leadership is needed in a club. Typically, saber clubs have three or more "instructors," or students of the sport who have mastered at least a few techniques and have their own copy of the training manual. In this way, any one of them can run a meeting. If you plan on being the sole instructor for all meetings to come, that can be an overwhelming amount of work, and lead to major issues. Worse still, if you are unexpectedly not able to run a meeting, club members may not know what to do, cancel the meeting, and leave the group. It is much better to establish a number of club leaders with set responsibilities. Type up these leadership roles, their matching responsibilities, and the schedule for your meetings. Make sure every leader of the club has a copy, and a copy is available online. Doing so will allow you to pass on these responsibilities easily to your successor in the future, as needed. If possible, it is best to decide all this before or just after your "Interest Meeting."

12. **Interest Meeting**: As curious people arrive at your first meeting, it helps to have refreshments and music playing in the background. Share your excitement and eagerly meet people, answering any questions they have as best you can. Don't forget to hand out your saber-smith recommendations. About 10 minutes after the start time, give a small presentation to the crowd. This can be an online video of thrilling fights, a demonstration of a duel between two of your starting members, or a preview-lesson presented by you and a friend of one of your favorite techniques. Most importantly, encourage everyone to join a social media page you have created for the group, and sign their names and email addresses on a lined sheet of paper. (This will help you contact them about cancelled meetings, changes in meeting location, and so forth.) In order to help your potential club members get the most out of their combat saber training, and access a number of awesome online resources, be sure to

also encourage them to create accounts with the Rogue Saber Academy.

13. **Weekly Meetings**: A typical club meeting can follow these steps, but you are free to adjust this schedule as you like:

- **First 5-10 minutes**: Club members stretch, warm up, and practice past learned techniques on their own. The club leaders should be friendly and ask individuals about their week and how their training has been going.

- **A Call to Order**: Club members are welcomed and encouraged to turn their attention to the instructor(s) in the Attentive Stance (as explained in Lesson 3 herein.) They may be reminded at this point about any membership fees, the need to sign-in, be given brief announcements, etc.

- **Quick review**: An instructor leads the whole group through the motions of previously learned techniques, and they are all demonstrated by the group, together, against imagined opponents. It is useful to give the name of the technique, a brief summary of it, and then give a clear signal to begin performing it with a countdown or similar prompt. Demonstrating certain movements repeatedly and frequently is encouraged to help club members retain what they have learned.

- **Swordsmanship Tip of the Week**: An instructor may take a brief moment to read a paragraph about the history behind these techniques, important safety standards, the duelists' code of honor, or some other non-movement-based lesson. Doing so can help encourage club members to maintain the proper attitude while training.

- **Instruction**: Two instructors (perhaps you and a friend who are always in charge, or two other members on a rotating list of volunteers) present the technique(s) of the week. This can easily be done as one instructor reads a technique while the other demonstrates it. Both instructors then take turns performing the maneuver against each other. All members are then encouraged to ready their sabers, and are walked through the instructions again, step by step, as a group. (Depending on the preferences of your group, it may be fun to invite a different club member to present the new lesson each week.)

- **Final Half**: The meeting can wrap up with a large chunk of time in which a limited number of students take turns to pair off (as space and attendance allows) in friendly spars. Perhaps official duels can also take place with an instructor keeping records on the outcome as part of an ongoing competition. As the end of the meeting draws near, call for the attention of your club members again, thank them for their attendance, and let them know when the next meeting will be.

14. **Special Events**: When certain milestones arrive in the year, (such as the end of a semester) and after your club members have had a good number of meetings to sharpen their skills, schedule public tournaments, demonstrations, and other events in which the student body or local public is invited as spectators. Follow the promotional steps discussed above as needed. Preparation for such events serves your club members by giving a reason to push themselves and a goal to reach. It also gives them a chance to feel satisfaction with their progress as they show what they have learned. Hosting such an event will also spread the word about your club and lead to more people coming to future meetings.

15. **Community Service**: Even if your club is not required to perform community service, it is still encouraged as a part of complete swordsmanship instruction. Remember, the terms "Samurai" and "Knight" have their roots in service to others. Students of the RSA perform charitable acts in order to advance in rank. Some suggestions and instructions on worthy projects can be found on the Rogue Order's webpage.

These suggestions come from the founders of the Rogue Saber Academy, based off their own experience starting and running community sports teams and school clubs. Nevertheless, feel free to tweak them in order to best serve your particular situation. Starting a club can be intimidating at first, but the friendships made and experiences gained are well worth it.

Starting your own club builds the community and makes tremendous strides for the growth and development of the sport. Keep up the good work, and good luck!

JOIN THE FIGHT – COMPETE IN THE CLAN WARS!

NOW THAT YOU ARE WELL-TRAINED in the arts of combat saber dueling, the time has come to choose a side and take a stand in the great CLAN WARS.

The wars are fought across countless duels by heroes, villains, champions, and usurpers. They are the magnificent battles between sworn enemies, across a history wrought by fragile alliances, shocking betrayal, clever strategy, and stories passed down the generations.

Year after year, the war rages on between the three clans of the Rogue Order, in a struggle as ancient as the sword itself. It is the legendary fight among the light, the dark, and balance. Among combat saber enthusiasts, there is no fiercer debate and no greater rivalry. Will the long-standing victors continue to prevail? Will the weakest clan finally overcome? The time has come for a single duelist to rise, and with the sparking clash of their glowing blade, change the fate of the Clan Wars forever...

Will you answer the call? Will you take your place in history? Now is the time to join the fight!

• • •

Any student who creates an account with the Rogue Saber Academy has the option to join a Dueling Clan of the Rogue Order of Knights. In this sport, your clan is like your family. It is comparable to your "house," "fraternity," or "home team." Each clan espouses different fundamental points of view and is filled with the most dedicated of students. Which clan will you join? Choose wisely:

GUARDIANS (Protectors from the Light side)

WARRIORS (Wielders of the Dark Side)

KEEPERS OF BALANCE (The Ones in the Middle)

As a member of a clan, you have exclusive clearance within the RSA's Duel Finder System to challenge rival clan members to "Clan War Duels." Winning such duels will increase the amount of WAR POINTS earned by your clan. On Saber-Day (April 4th) of each year, the points earned by each clan are totaled, and a winner is declared. All members of the winning clan receive a number of prizes, including a large amount of digital Duel Credits, and the eternal honor, glory, and bragging rights of having their clan's victory immortalized in the records of the RSA.

If you have made it this far in your training, participating in the Clan Wars is a great way to experience some of the fierceness and competitive edge that gave rise to the techniques you have mastered. It is also tremendous fun, and certainly worth a try!

BIBLIOGRAPHY

WHILE OVER A YEAR was spent by the author studying and reading any and all guides on Japanese Swordsmanship within reach, and on fencing in general, the following books and resources in particular proved indispensable in the research process, and clearly captured the spirit of their respective arts. To their authors and publishers, the sincerest of gratitude is owed. For students, the following list provides an excellent collection to help you continue your training:

Cohen, Richard. *By the Sword: a History of Gladiators, Musketeers, Samurai, Swashbucklers, and Olympic Champions.* The Modern Library, 2012.

Daidoji, Yuzan. *Budoshoshinshu: the Warrior's Primer.* Edited by Jack Vaughn. Translated by Scott Wilson, Ohara, 1987.

De Lange, William, et al. *Iaido: History, Teaching & Practice Of Japanese Swordsmanship.* Weatherhill, 2002.

Imafuji, Hiro. "Traditional Kendo Instructions." *Kendo For Life*, Kendo For Life LLC, www.kendo-for-life.com.

Miyamoto, Musashi, et al. *The Illustrated Book of Five Rings.* Weatherhill, 2006.

Salmon, Geoff. *Kendo: a Comprehensive Guide to Japanese Swordsmanship.* Tuttle Publishing, 2013.

Wallace, Daniel. *The Jedi Path: A Manual for Students of the Force.* Chronicle Books LLC, 2016.

Yoshida, Kohshyu. *Samurai Sword: Spirit Strategy Techniques.* Tuttle Publishing, 2010.

ACKNOWLEDGEMENTS

HEART-FELT THANKS and the deepest feelings of friendship go out to all those with a hand in making this book possible.

The saber-smiths and academy masters out there who developed such an amazing weapon and the sport to go with it.

Wesley Freeman and the first students and Beta Testers of the RSA's website. Your suggestions and input fueled the fire of the academy's growth like nothing else could.

My first *senseis* of the Palouse Kendo Club, and Hiro Imafuji, for answering all my bizarre questions, and for showing such dedication to the art.

The very first circle of friends awesome enough to start an academy with us – Haley, Devin, and Caitlyn.

Rebecca, for being the excellent human being that she is.

Connie, my best friend, for her support from the beginning, for the countless bruises and long weekends sparring, and for being both a dedicated student, a masterful teacher, and the kind of person all others wish to be.

And to you, the reader. Thank you for the role you play in the growth of this community, and for your honest online review of this book.

NOTES

Made in the USA
Monee, IL
29 October 2020

46361759R00164